Scottish Fairy Tales, Myths & Legends

Published in the UK by Scholastic Children's Books, 2020
Euston House, 24 Eversholt Street, London, NW1 1DB, UK
A division of Scholastic Limited.

London – New York – Toronto – Sydney – Auckland
Mexico City – New Delhi – Hong Kong

ISBN 978-93-5471-923-3

A CIP catalogue record for this book
is available from the British Library.

www.scholastic.co.uk

First edition 2020
This reprint edition June 2024

Printed in India at Shivam Offset Press, New Delhi

Scottish
Fairy
Tales,
Myths &
Legends
Mairi
Kidd
SCHOLASTIC

Contents

Monsters, Magical Creatures and Shapeshifters

Scotland and Ireland and Scandinavia

For Olivia & Chloe

Introduction

"A good tale never tires in the telling"

—SCOTTISH PROVERB

Anywhere people gather, stories are told. People pass on gossip or tell one another what's in the news.

Long ago, before television and the internet, recorded sound and the printed word, storytelling was an important way of bringing communities together. People told stories to entertain one another, to share knowledge and to spark the imagination of listeners. Some people had a special gift for storytelling, and they passed stories down to other tellers, cherished and polished like precious jewels.

While the tradition of passing down stories in this way still exists in Scotland in the present day, it is rarer now. As long as two hundred years ago, collectors began to see that many stories would be lost if they were not recorded. They began to write them down, and, as technology developed, to record them too. Many of the stories in this book come from the great collections of the nineteenth and twentieth centuries, and hopefully they will come to life in your mind's eye as you read on.

Once upon a time. . .

Famous Fairy Tales, Scottish-Style

A Scottish Riddle

I am a little barrel without a base
I hold blood and flesh and bone
What am I?

Answer
A ring

Stories have bones and flesh, and sometimes they even have blood in them (but only if the characters are unlucky). The bones of a story are the steps that take it from *once upon a time* to *happily ever after.* The flesh is all the detail that brings the story to life.

Fairy tales often share their bones with stories

from all around the world. The flesh may be different, but the bones are the same.

Once upon a time, a storyteller in Greece told the story of a serving girl whose slipper was stolen by an eagle. The eagle dropped the slipper in the lap of the king, who sent messengers far and wide to seek the girl whose foot it fit to become his wife.

Once upon another time, a storyteller in China told of a girl called Ye Xian, whose mother dies and comes back to advise her as a magical fish. When she flees from a festival, losing her tiny golden slipper, the king of a nearby island vows to marry none but the girl who fits the shoe.

Once upon a time, a French writer called Charles Perrault told a story about a girl with a wicked stepmother and a fairy godmother, a slipper of glass and a pumpkin coach. He called the girl – of course – Cinderella.

The first story in this chapter shares the same bones as "Cinderella", but with different flesh. In fact, all of the fairy tales in this chapter share their bones with famous stories. How many do you recognize?

The Cat-Faced Lady

This is a story from the Gaelic tradition of the Highlands. It is very like a famous story told in French by Charles Perrault, in German by the Brothers Grimm, and in English by many people, including Walt Disney. Perhaps you might recognize it. As is often the case in Gaelic stories, there is a character called the Hen Wife. In some stories she is a witch, but here she is an unkind stepmother without any magical powers at all.

Once upon a time there was a good nobleman whose wife was as lovely as the summer sun, and as kind as the month of May. The couple had one daughter, and she was just as lovely and as kind as her mother.

This little family lived very happily until a sad day came when the nobleman's wife died. The nobleman and his daughter's hearts were broken. They mourned her for a year and a day, and then the nobleman decided that he should marry again. He wished his daughter to have a new mother, for he knew that she sorely missed her own.

The woman the nobleman married was called the Hen Wife. She was a widow with three daughters. These daughters were as awful as the nobleman's daughter was lovely, and as mean as she was kind. From the moment they first laid eyes on their step-sister, they envied and resented and despised her.

Not long after the marriage, the king went to war in a distant land and the nobleman had to do his duty and go off with the army. Before he left he asked the Hen Wife to promise to look after his daughter as though she were her own.

"What a silly thing to ask," said the Hen Wife. "You know I will."

This put the nobleman's mind quite at ease. He gave a purse of gold to the Hen Wife and told her to send his daughter to school, so that she might grow into a great and wise lady in her own right.

The Hen Wife accepted the money, but she made sure the nobleman's daughter never saw the inside of a schoolroom. As soon as her husband had mounted his horse and ridden off, the Hen Wife made a servant of his daughter. Instead of learning calculus and composition and calligraphy, the girl had to clean and sweep and wait on the Hen Wife's daughters. Those bullies were delighted with this turn of events, and they kept their stepsister on her feet from dawn to dusk, running to and fro to iron their dresses and shine their shoes and fetch whatever it was that they wanted.

Far, far away in the land of Greece, the king's son had come of age. His father wished him to marry, but the prince had no interest in marrying at all. The king kept on and on and on at him, and in the end the prince gave in.

"I will only marry," said the prince, "the loveliest girl in the world."

The prince thought this was terribly clever, for who on earth could ever prove that they had found the loveliest girl in the world? Who could ever be certain of a thing like that?

The king was not so daft.

"Very well," said he. "Off you go and find that girl." Then he turned to his wife. "That'll teach him," he said. "Now he'll have to set off and travel the world. Much better than lazing around in bed half the day."

The king was right. The lad had no choice but to set out to travel the world. He took along a knight as his travelling companion. At each town they reached, the knight would march into the inn and tell all gathered there that the King of Greece's son had come in search of the loveliest girl in the world to be his wife.

A great ball would be called and every woman and girl in the place would array herself in her finest clothes in hope of catching the prince's eye. In this way the prince met hundreds upon hundreds upon hundreds of girls. Every one seemed less interesting than the last, and he was no closer to finding a girl to marry.

After a year and a day, the prince and the knight came to the town where the nobleman's house was. When the Hen Wife heard there was to be a ball in three days' time, she almost burst with joy. There was no doubt in her mind that the prince would marry one of her three daughters.

The nobleman's daughter was desperate to go to the ball, but the Hen Wife would not let her. Instead, they put her to work filling the bath over and over, ironing all their dresses, styling their hair and painting make-up on their awful faces, while the daughters squabbled endlessly among themselves about which one the prince would marry. Of course, they never spared a thought for their stepsister. What possible business could a scruffy serving girl have at a royal ball? If they'd seen that her heart was breaking, they'd have teased and mocked her, and so she kept her sorrow to herself.

At last, the night of the ball arrived, and the Hen Wife and her daughters departed in a coach paid for with the nobleman's gold. His own daughter was left alone at home. She was so tired and so lonely that she sat down on the floor and began to weep. After a little while, she fell asleep.

When the girl woke up, the fire had gone out and the house was as cold as poison.

Long ago, people would only allow their fire to go out on one night of the year, at the great festival of Beltane. Even then they would keep one ember aglow, to bring the fire to life again. The nobleman's daughter had no idea how to light a fire when it had gone black and cold, and she was terrified that she had brought great bad luck upon the house. And so she pulled her shawl around her and ran to the house of the cat-faced lady.

The reason for the cat-faced lady's odd name was that the left half of her face looked like the face of a cat, with one green eye and one wide cheekbone, one pointed tooth and one pointed ear. Everyone said she was a witch, and some went out of their way not to pass close by her house at night for fear of what they might see. The nobleman's daughter was a little afraid of witchcraft and magic, but she knew that the cat-faced lady was wise and would know how to bring the fire to life again.

"Why aren't you at the ball?" the cat-faced lady asked, when she saw the nobleman's daughter at her door. "I understood that the King of Greece's son wished to meet every girl in the land."

"I think so," the girl said, "but the Hen Wife says that I am a serving girl, and no one takes serving girls with them when they go to a ball." She stole a shy look at the witch. "When they left I fell asleep, and the fire went out. Do you know how to bring it to life again?"

"Why, certainly," said the cat-faced lady, and she lifted a burning ember from the fire with her tongs. "Take this home now," she said, "and use it to bring the fire to life. When you have the fire going again, come back here to me. You're not a servant, you're a nobleman's daughter. And, anyway, *every* girl has the right to go to the ball."

The girl had no idea why the cat-faced lady wanted her to return, but she was grateful for the ember, and so when the fire had roared back into life, she smoored it down and ran back to the witch's house.

"Close the door," said the cat-faced lady, and she took out a magic wand. She tapped the girl with the wand and her ragged dress turned into a gown made of every colour of the rainbow. Her old boots turned into glass slippers and a crown of diamonds appeared on her head

The cat-faced lady ushered the girl outside and down to the gable end of the house, where an old dog and a donkey stood waiting. She tapped the donkey with her wand, and in a heartbeat it became a white mare with silver shoes, a leather saddle and silken drapes. The dog became a servant in a suit of silk with golden buttons.

The nobleman's daughter stared and stared in

wonder, until the witch took her by the arm and helped her on to the horse. “Have a good evening,” she said. “Now, you must remember that the magic only lasts until midnight. Whatever happens, you must leave before then.”

When the girl arrived at the ball, the dance floor was full. But when she stepped into the room, every dancer turned to stare. It wasn’t her rainbow gown or her glistening jewels or her shining shoes that drew them – they only had eyes for her lovely face. Who was she? No one had the slightest idea.

The prince asked her to dance. They spun around and around the floor for dance after dance, all the other guests forgotten. The prince had never met a girl who spoke to his heart like this one. The nobleman’s daughter had never met a man so thoughtful or so kind.

Then midnight came – and she was gone.

No one spoke of anything else all night.

The Hen Wife and her daughters were still jabbering with fury when they came home in the small hours of the morning. They sat and ate the food the girl had prepared and wailed and moaned and lamented. The Greek king’s son had been poached from under their noses by a nobody!

The prince was not in a much better mood. The loveliest girl on earth had been in his arms, and she had run from him before the night was over. He made the knight announce another ball, in the hope of enticing her there again.

The ball was called and the country was alive with the news. The women were all a-fluster finding new gowns and shoes and jewels to wear to this new occasion. They had all already been seen in their best.

The nobleman's daughter's heart was heavy. Her tummy tingled when she remembered the prince, but her stepsisters gave her not a minute's peace to gather her thoughts. They made her sew a new dress for each of them, and knit new stockings and trim new shoes with jewels. She slept not a wink for three days and three nights until the costumes were done. When they finally rode off to the ball, she collapsed by the fire and slept. And when she woke, the fire was out.

The girl took herself to the house of the cat-faced lady.

"Why aren't you at the ball?" the witch asked. "I heard the prince was very enamoured of a lady in a gown of rainbows."

The nobleman's daughter blushed. "I have nothing to wear to a ball," she said. "Not even the rainbow gown, for that disappeared with the other magic."

"Go home and light the fire," said the witch. "And then return here to me."

The girl did as she was asked. When she returned, the cat-faced lady took up her wand again, and turned the girl's old dress into a gown of feathers. No two feathers were alike, and they glowed with every colour in creation. Pearl shoes shone on her feet.

Outside, the donkey and the dog were waiting. The cat-faced lady tapped them with the wand, and the servant and the mare appeared. The girl climbed on to the mare and rode to the ball.

When the nobleman's daughter appeared in the doorway, the dancing stopped in an instant. But although the guests studied her face, no one knew her and they had no idea where she had come from. They fell back, and the Greek king's son stepped forward. They danced, and he did not let her go. Her heart was torn, but she knew that at the stroke of midnight all her glory would be gone and the prince would find himself holding a servant in his arms. She could not bear to see him turn from her. And so, before the clock struck twelve, she slipped from his arms and out of the hall.

The prince was desperate, and he insisted on calling another ball before the night was out. The Hen Wife and her daughters came home and spoke of nothing else but the mysterious girl who had appeared at the ball and behaved so strangely, disappearing again before midnight.

"I'll bet you," said the Hen Wife, "that she's married to someone else."

"Maybe," said the daughters, and they cheered up a little.

Now every girl in the land was fighting over the last pieces of cloth in the land to make yet another set of gowns fit for a ball. The Hen Wife's daughters made their stepsister sew them dresses of gold cloth and silver thread. By the time they left for the ball, her hands were raw and sore. She fell asleep, and once more she had to return to the witch's house for embers to kindle the fire.

This time the cat-faced lady made her a gown of the night sky, with the moon and the stars shining among its folds, and shoes of diamond. She rode to the ball, and when she arrived the prince was waiting anxiously at the door. He took her in and he would not let her out of his sight. She wished and wished that she could tell him her secret, but she knew she could not, and so she settled for dreaming that the night would never end. When the first strike of midnight sounded, her heart leaped in her chest. She tore herself from him and ran from the room. In her haste she dropped one of her diamond slippers. The prince stumbled over it as he chased her. When he righted himself, she was gone.

The prince gave the shoe to the knight.

"We will visit every house in this land," he said, "and we will not rest until we find the girl whose foot fits this slipper, for she is the loveliest in the world, and I will marry none but her."

The Hen Wife's daughters were sick with nerves when they heard that the prince was on his way to their house with the diamond shoe. They pulled on their best gowns and jostled and pushed at one another as each fought to be first to meet him. As the nobleman's daughter followed behind, the Hen Wife grabbed her by the arm and looked her full in the face for the first time since they had met all those months before.

"Well," said the Hen Wife. "We can't have a dirty serving girl ruining the day for the prince."

She dragged the nobleman's daughter to the larder, pushed her inside and locked the door.

One by one, the Hen Wife's daughters tried on the shoe. The first one's feet were too long, and though she cut her toenails and pushed and pulled, it would not fit. The second daughter's feet were too wide, and though she rammed and jammed until the little bones in her feet creaked with the strain, the shoe would not fit. The feet of the third weren't so wide or so long as her sisters', and after she cut her nails and pushed and pulled and rammed and jammed, the shoe at last went on.

The prince wasn't pleased – he knew this wasn't the girl he had fallen in love with – but he had given his word and it seemed that he had no choice but to marry the Hen Wife's third daughter. The Hen Wife was delighted. Her other daughters were green with envy, and the nobleman's daughter was sick with grief.

On the day of the wedding, the Hen Wife left the nobleman's daughter at home cleaning and sweeping and preparing for the feast. When the bride and her mother rode off in the bridal party, the girl sat down by the fire and she began to cry.

The prince and the knight rode in the bridal

procession with heavy hearts. When they were halfway to church, a bird flew above them all and sang:

"That foot there in the stirrup
is swollen and bruised.
Another should wear the shoe;
the daughter much abused."

"Did you hear that?" the prince asked.

"No," said the Hen Wife. "I heard bird twitter, that's all."

She tugged on the prince's reins to pull him on, but the bird sang on:

"Swollen and bruised. . .
the daughter much abused. . ."

The prince turned his horse and made for the nobleman's house. By the fire he found the nobleman's daughter, and he lifted her into his arms.

"I'd know you anywhere," he said. "The loveliest girl in all the world."

"Lovely? In these rags?" said the nobleman's daughter.

"Would you not love me in rags?" asked the prince.

"I would," said the nobleman's daughter, and her heart swelled with happiness, for she knew it was true. She would love him until the seas ran dry, and he loved her just as truly.

The nobleman came home from the war for his daughter's wedding. When he heard what the Hen Wife and her daughters had done, he cast them out.

No one forgot the cat-faced lady's kindness. She never needed her magic again, for the nobleman's daughter gave her a horse and a coach, a fine house and silk gowns and more food than she could eat in two lifetimes.

The Well at the World's End

This is a story from the Scottish Borders, and it was told on the English side of the border too. A version was recorded by the Australian collector Joseph Jacobs in a book called English Fairy Tales *in 1890, but he found it in a much older book called the* Complaynt of Scotland, *written in 1549. It is another tale known in various forms the world over.*

The well in the story would not look like a wishing well, but rather a natural spring in the ground.

Once upon a time, there lived a girl whose mother had died. The girl and her father grieved the loss full sore, but in time their sorrow began to lessen, and the father saw his way to marrying again. The woman he married hated her new husband's daughter, for she saw that the girl was more beautiful than she, and it turned her heart quite cold with bitterness. She took every chance she had to be cruel to her stepdaughter, and the chances she had were many, for soon her husband went off to war and left her in charge of the house. She wasted no time in making a servant out of her stepdaughter, forcing her to fetch and carry and answer her every whim. Still the stepmother's cruel heart was not satisfied and she began to think of ways to be rid of her stepdaughter for ever. In the end she hit on a plan she thought most cunning indeed.

The girl was sitting in the sunshine with her mending one fine morning when she felt a shadow come over the day. She shivered and turned to see her stepmother standing behind her, blocking out the sun. She had a sieve in her hand and she held it out to the girl.

"Take this sieve," her stepmother said, "and go to the Well at the World's End. Fill the sieve from the well and bring the water home to me. Woe betide you if you do not bring it home to me full to the brim."

The girl was, in truth, afraid of her stepmother and so she took the sieve, rushed to pack some food and belongings in a shawl, and set out to find the Well at the World's End. She had never heard of any such well and had no idea where to start looking for it, but it seemed that was the least of her troubles. For how could anyone bring water home in a sieve?

The girl walked along the road and into the mountains, and every time she passed a traveller, she asked if they knew the way to the Well at the World's End. No one did, and some of them laughed at the question. In this manner she walked for a week and a day, until at last she met an old woman, bent almost in two and leaning on a stick. She took pity on the woman, and she invited her to share the last of the oatcakes and cheese she had brought in her pack.

"Such a kind girl you are," said the old woman. "I was very hungry, for I have just returned from the Well at the World's End. The water there is so pure and so cold, and even though I had only a thimbleful of it to drink, it did my old heart more good than any other thing on earth."

The girl's heart leaped with excitement. "I want to visit the well too," she cried. "But I don't know where to look."

"It is hard to find," said the old woman, "for almost no one goes there now and so it is hidden by the bright green grass, and the path that leads to it is under bracken." She took the girl's hands and looked into her eyes. The girl looked past the lines of age on the old woman's face, and saw how the sparkle of water shone in her eyes, water that could heal any hurt, even the hurt of the heart.

The next thing the girl knew, the old woman was gone, and she stood in a place she had never seen before, beside a dancing well. For a few happy seconds the girl felt delight bubble up through her. She fell to her knees and dipped her sieve in the cold water, but it all just ran through. She tried again and again, but every time it was the same. At last the girl sat down and cried, feeling that her heart had broken. The task was surely impossible; she could never go home again.

"Excuse me, madam?" a croaky voice said by her ear.

The girl leaped nearly a foot in the air with shock.

When her heart stilled, she looked around, but she could not see who had spoken.

"Hello?" she said. "Who's there?"

"Down here," the voice said, and the girl looked down. A frog stood among the rushes by the well. "What's the matter, my dear?" it asked.

"My stepmother has sent me all this way to bring her home water from this well," the girl said, "but I have only a sieve to carry it, and I can't find any way to do it at all."

"I can help you," said the frog, "but in return I must ask you a favour."

"Anything," said the girl.

"You must promise to do what I ask for a whole night long," said the frog. "Then I'll tell you how to fill it."

What harm can a frog do me? the girl thought, and so she agreed, and the frog said,

> *"Stop it with moss and daub it with clay,*
> *And then it will carry the water away."*

Then the frog gave a hop, a skip and a jump, and it disappeared into the Well at the World's End. The girl watched him go, hoping he had forgotten her promise and she would never see the strange creature again.

The girl searched for moss to line the sieve, and when she had done that she gathered handfuls of clay and spread it over the moss. Then she dipped the sieve into the well water, and the sieve filled up.

The girl set out for home, careful not to spill a drop from the sieve, and at last she reached home and gave the water to her stepmother.

Her stepmother had never expected to see the girl again, for who knew if there even was a well at the world's end, and even if anyone could find it, surely no one could carry water home in a sieve? She was furious, but she didn't let on.

That night, as the girl dozed and the stepmother nursed her fury by the fire, they heard a knock at the door and a voice said,

> *"Open the door, my henny, my heart,*
> *Open the door, my own darling;*
> *Mind you the words that you and I spake,*
> *Down in the meadow, at the World's End Well."*

The girl knew that it must be the frog, and she told her stepmother what she had promised. The thought of her stepdaughter waiting hand and foot on a slimy old frog cheered the stepmother up a little, and she smiled a nasty smile and asked the frog to come in. It hopped into the room and jumped up to the girl, and it said,

"Lift me to your knee, my henny, my heart;
Lift me to your knee, my own darling;
Remember the words that you and I spake,
Down in the meadow, by the World's End Well."

"Lift the frog up this instant, you insolent creature!" said the stepmother. "Girls must keep their promises!"

The girl shuddered at the thought of touching the frog, but she composed herself and lifted it on to her lap. Then it said,

"Give me some supper, my henny, my heart,
Give me some supper, my darling;
Remember the words that you and I spake,
Down in the meadow, by the World's End Well."

The girl fetched the frog a bowl of milk and bread, and it ate its fill. When it had finished, it said,

"Go with me to bed, my henny, my heart,
Go with me to bed, my own darling;
Remember the words that you and I spake,
Down in the meadow, by the World's End Well."

The stepmother cackled with delight at the thought of the slimy frog in the girl's clean sheets. "Girls must keep their promises," she sneered. "Nighty night, my dear! Nighty night, froggie!"

And so the girl had no choice but to take the frog to her chamber and lay it on the bed. She climbed in and sat all night watching it. Just as dawn broke the frog said,

"Chop off my head, my henny, my heart,
Chop off my head, my own darling;
Remember the words that you and I spake,
Down in the meadow, by the World's End Well."

"I can't do that!" said the girl. "What a way to repay your kindness to me at the well!"

But the frog kept on and on, and in the end the girl got a knife and she chopped off the frog's head. And as soon as the head was off the frog disappeared, and a handsome prince stood before the girl. She listened in wonder as the prince told her how he had been bewitched by a wicked magician, and the spell could not be broken until a girl would agree to do his bidding for a whole night, and end it by cutting off his head in the morning.

The stepmother was wild with fury when she saw the prince and heard the story. But the prince and the girl didn't care; they said that they were to be married and that was that, and the stepmother could like it or she could lump it. One thing was sure, and that was that they would never see her again because they were going to go and live in his father's castle and be waited on hand and foot.

The stepmother had to live with the knowledge that through her cruelty she had brought about her stepdaughter's great happiness. She began to worry that her husband would return from war, discover her treachery and throw her out, and with every day that passed, this worry weighed more heavily upon her, until it bent her almost in two. The girl and the prince gave her never a thought, but lived happily ever after in a love like the water of the well, that healed all hurts, even the hurts of the heart.

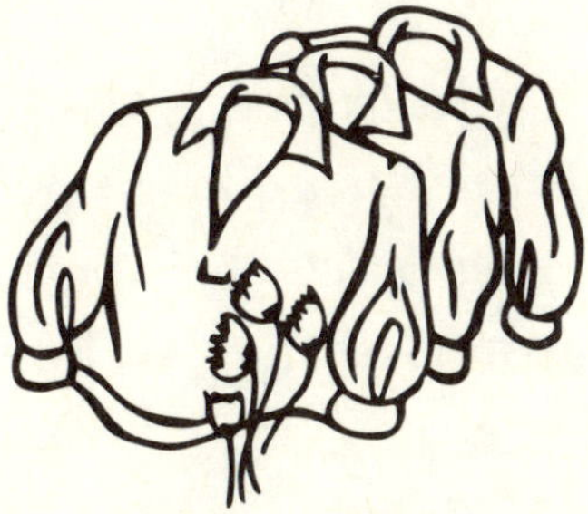

The Three Shirts of Bog-cotton

This story is found in many countries across the world. There is a particularly famous version from Ireland, and the great Danish writer Hans Christian Andersen wrote a version of his own that has been loved by many hundreds of thousands of readers, young and old. This particular telling is inspired by the great Gaelic storyteller Duncan MacDonald of Peninerine, in the island of South Uist, where the white fluffy plant known as bog-cotton is a common sight. The achievements of the heroine of the story seem even greater when you know that it is almost impossible to spin the fibres of its seed pods into cloth.

In the story, a witch appears who is known as the

"Eachlair Ùrlar". No teller of tales today knows precisely where this name came from – perhaps it derives from a character in older beliefs. It is pronounced "Echlar Oorlar" (say the "ch" as Scottish people say it in the word "loch").

Once upon a time there lived a king who knew all the happiness in the world, for he had loyal subjects, a loving wife, three strong sons and a clever daughter. But then his wife died, and for a time the light dimmed in the king's heart. When at last he recovered himself a little, he saw that there were dark circles under his children's eyes, and the house was grey and drab where once it had glowed with joy. He made up his mind that he should find another wife – a young, kindly woman who would care for the children and bring love and laughter to their lives again. Indeed, not long after the new queen arrived, the circles vanished from under the children's eyes, their cheeks grew rosy and once again the house rang with song and laughter.

Then, one day, the Eachlair Ùrlar came to the house. She was a witch, and she wasted no time in asking the new queen how she was getting along with the children.

"The little loves," said the queen. "It's as if they were my own."

"Foolish, foolish, foolish," said the witch. "What if the king died tomorrow? Or if you had children of your own? You'd inherit nothing, and your children would inherit nothing. The first wife's brats would have it all."

The witch kept on in this manner for days and weeks, until she had driven all other thoughts out of the queen's head.

"But what should I do?" the queen asked. "I could never harm the children. Never."

"You don't have to do anything," said the witch. "Just send them up to my house, one by one. Tell them you want them to bring you my yellow comb."

The next day the queen sent the eldest boy to the witch's house. "Tell her," she said, "that your stepmother has sent you for her yellow comb."

The boy set out in good spirits and made his way to the witch's house, where he knocked and went in. He said that his stepmother had sent him to fetch a yellow comb.

"The comb is on the dresser over there, my darling," said the witch. "Take it."

As soon the boy's back was turned, the witch picked up a wand she kept by her. She struck the boy with it, and he was turned into a great black raven. The witch laughed and laughed.

The raven flew out of the house. As he crossed the threshold, he spat out a mouthful of blood on the step.

Back home they waited and waited, but the eldest boy didn't return, and so the queen sent the next eldest to the witch's house to look for his brother.

"Have you seen my brother today?" he asked. "My stepmother sent him to ask for a yellow comb."

"I haven't seen hide nor hair of him," said the witch, "but there's the comb on the dresser. Go on, sweet lad – take it."

As the boy picked up the comb, she struck him with her wand and he was turned into another black raven. He flew around the house and out of the door, and as he passed the threshold he saw the mark of blood on the stone. He spat out another mouthful beside it. The witch laughed and laughed.

Now both boys were missing and the queen sent the youngest boy to the witch's house to tell his brothers to come home immediately.

"I haven't seen anyone today, my little love," said the witch. "But there's the comb on the dresser." And again she turned him into a raven. As he flew out of the house, he spat a third mouthful of blood on the doorstep. The witch laughed and laughed.

Now all three boys were missing, and the queen went to find their sister.

"Every one of your brothers has defied me," she

complained. "I asked them to run an errand and they've gone off somewhere to play. You need to go to the Eachlair Ùrlair's house to fetch me her yellow comb. And bring those boys home if you meet them on the way."

When the girl arrived at the house, the door was closed. She knocked, and as she waited, she saw three small spots on the doorstep that looked like blood.

What on earth has happened here today? she said to herself.

The girl went in and asked the witch if she had seen her brothers.

"No, indeed, my little warrior lass," said the witch, and she laughed a laugh that grated in the girl's ears. "But I have the yellow comb for your stepmother over there, on the dresser."

The girl was older than her brothers, and a little more suspicious, and as she walked over to the dresser, she kept an eye on the witch. When she saw her pick up her wand, she leaped on her and wrestled it from her hands. As they struggled, the witch was struck in the face and turned into a pillar of stone.

She wasn't laughing now.

The girl sat down at the table and tried to calm her pounding heart. It was growing dark, and when night had fallen full and black and still, the door opened and her brothers came in, in human form once more. The girl leaped to her feet and embraced them.

"What happened to you?" she asked.

"We're under a spell," the eldest told her. "She turned us into ravens. From sunrise until sunset, we will take bird form for the rest of our lives."

"Our stepmother must have known," said the middle brother. "She sent us here."

"You can't go home," said the youngest. "It isn't safe."

The girl felt as though her heart would break but she took a deep breath and squared her shoulders. "Surely there's something I can do to free you from the spell?" she said.

"One thing," said the eldest brother. "But it's impossible."

The girl raised her chin and glared at him, daring him to dismiss her determination. "I'll be the judge of that," she said.

Her brothers explained that she would have to make them each a shirt from the plant called bog-cotton. She would have to pluck it and card it and spin it, and weave the cloth and sew the shirts.

"But from the day you begin to harvest the bog-cotton," her eldest brother said, "until the day you say, 'fine health to wear this shirt, my brother,' you may say not one word to a living soul. If you do, we will be ravens for ever."

The girl nodded. "Well," she said, "I'd better get started."

She began the very next day. She took all she needed from the witch's house and she plucked three sackfuls of bog-cotton on the first day. On the second day she plucked three more, and by the end of the third she had nine sacks full. By then she was so tired that she lay down by the side of the road in the shelter of the sacks and fell asleep.

The girl woke in the black arch of night. A man's voice was speaking to her from the darkness. At first her heart pounded in her chest, but the voice was kind.

"Are you quite well?" the voice asked. "Are you lost?"

She looked at him but she said nothing.

"Poor creature," the voice said. "Don't be afraid; you're safe now." Then she heard a snapping of fingers, and a servant appeared carrying a lantern. She was scooped up and carried into a carriage, where she was set on a seat of silk and covered in a quilt of satin.

The girl awoke the next morning in a beautiful chamber where warm water, fine clothes and good food were laid ready for her and a serving girl waited to help her. When she was dressed and fed, there was a knock at the door and a nobleman entered. She recognized his voice at once and opened her mouth to say thank you, but then she closed it again just as quickly.

"I reckon she can't speak, sir," said the serving girl.

Now the girl had remembered her task, and her heart fluttered in her chest. She looked in panic at the nobleman, and he offered her his hand. He took her to the next chamber, where her sacks were waiting, and a spindle and a loom and everything else she needed to work the cotton.

For long months the girl lived in the nobleman's house and worked on the first shirt, carding and combing and spinning the bog-cotton into thread. At first the nobleman tried to make her speak, but as the months wore on he accepted that she could not. Still he came to sit with her whenever he could, and told her all the thoughts in his head, and she listened with joy, for she had grown to love this man who had been so kind to her. And then one day he told her the wishes of his heart, and although she could not speak, she found she could nod, and in this way she agreed to be his wife.

By the time they married the spinning was done, and after the wedding she began the weaving and then the cutting and sewing. The very night she finished the first shirt, folded it and put it away in a kist in her room, her first child was born – a son. The nobleman was as joyful as a lark on the wing. He sat up late with his friends and brothers while his wife and the midwife slumbered upstairs.

In the grey light of dawn, the nobleman crept into his wife's chamber and peeked into the cradle to see his sleeping son. But the baby wasn't in the cradle. He wasn't with his mother in bed. He wasn't with the midwife where she slept in a chair. He wasn't anywhere. A frantic search turned up nothing and no one could offer any explanation, least of all the child's mother. He seemed to have been spirited away, as if by magic.

When she had recovered her health if not her

happiness, the girl went with heavy steps and a heavier heart to the outer room and began the work of making the second shirt, carding, combing and spinning the cotton, and weaving, cutting and sewing the cloth. On the very night the second shirt was finished, folded and put away, her second son was born.

This time they were determined to stay awake. But the night was dark and the room was warm, and the worry had weighed so heavily on them for so long. By the early hours of the morning, they had all fallen asleep. And when they woke in the light of day, the baby was gone.

Even though the nobleman had been in the room, he could no more offer an explanation for the disappearance than anyone else. And so they grieved and others whispered, and after a while had passed the girl went with a tear-stained face and a broken heart to the outer room and began work on the carding and spinning for the third shirt. And the very night she sewed the last stitch, folded the shirt and put it away, her third son was born.

Again the nobleman was determined to make sure absolutely nothing could happen to the baby. He stayed awake all night past dawn while the others slumbered. But as the grey morning light kissed the window, his head slumped forward and he slept. When he woke, the baby was gone.

Now the whispers grew into roars. The girl was unnatural, the people shouted, without speech to tell them who she was or where she came from. They said that she would have to answer for the disappearance of the children, and if she would not or could not, she would have to pay for it with her life.

The nobleman begged and pleaded, but the people were determined to take his wife from the house. As they dragged her to the door, someone shouted in surprise. Three masked riders had just reined in their horses outside the house. Each one held a child in front of him on the saddle. One child was around two years old, the second perhaps a year, and the third was a newborn baby.

The three riders dismounted and the people saw that they were not yet grown men. The tallest of them spoke to the nobleman.

"May we speak with your wife?"

"You may speak to her," the nobleman said, "but she cannot speak to you. I wish she could."

The nobleman took the horsemen and his wife

into the house and closed the door on the crowd outside.

The girl led the way to the outer chamber of her rooms and opened the kist in the corner. She took out the three shirts she had made and shook them out.

"Fine health to wear this shirt, sweet brother," she said, and she handed her eldest brother the first shirt.

"Fine health to you, loyal sister," he said, "and here is your eldest son. We have cared for him for you."

The girl hugged the child to her and handed him to his father. It was the nobleman's turn to be struck dumb.

"Fine health to wear this shirt, sweet brother," she said to her middle brother, and handed him the second shirt.

"Fine health to you, loyal sister," he said, "and here is your second son."

The girl hugged the child to her and gave him to his father. Tears ran down the nobleman's face.

"Fine health to wear this shirt, sweet brother," she said for the last time, and she handed her youngest brother the last shirt.

"Fine health to you, loyal sister," he said, "and here is your son who was born last night."

The girl took the baby and the nobleman hugged her as best he could with two children in his own arms and they cried as the brothers told him about the witch's curse and all that their sister had done to help them.

"We are so sorry," the youngest brother said. "We cared for the children tenderly, but we could not leave them with you. Just think, had one stumbled too near the fire. You would have called out. We would never have been returned to human form."

"I understand," said the girl. "I wanted to save you. It was my choice."

"It wasn't mine," said the nobleman, "but how could I have known?"

The nobleman had his servants water the brothers' horses and prepare the carriage, and the very next day they set out for their father's house. They found their father dying, a broken man, having lost his children long years before. When he beheld them again, he rose from his bed for the first time in weeks and embraced them. They told him of the queen's deceit and the witch's treachery, and the king vowed to cast the queen out and have the witch thrown into the sea.

The girl and her husband stayed with her family until her father had quite recovered. At first they found it difficult to talk and were tongue-tied with one another, but soon they discovered there were not enough words to tell of the joy in their hearts. When the king was quite well again, they bid him farewell and returned home with their little family to live together quite happily for the rest of their lives. The brothers remained at home, and they never forgot to be thankful for the strength of their sister's love.

Lasair Gheug, the King of Ireland's Daughter

This is another story from Gaelic tradition, and although many of the details are different, you are certain to know its most famous version, which comes from the telling of the Brothers Grimm. This version is set in Ireland and "Lochlann", which means all of the lands the Vikings lived in. Really it is set, like most Gaelic wonder-tales, in a fairy tale never-never land.

The heroine's name, Lasair Gheug, means "Slender Flame". It is pronounced "Lasser Yayg". The Hen Wife is back again, but this time she is a witch, poisoning the heart of a stepmother who starts out kind and loving.

The King and Queen of Ireland had one daughter who was as lovely and as merry as a dancing flame, and so they named her Lasair Gheug. Lasair Gheug's light dimmed for a time when her mother died, but the king saw how mournful she was and how she longed for a mother's love, and he determined that he should marry again. The new queen loved Lasair Gheug dearly and treated her as kindly as she would her own daughter.

But then, one day, the Hen Wife came to the house. She was a witch, and she saw how things were between the queen and Lasair Gheug.

"You shouldn't be so kind to that brat," said the witch. "What if the king died tomorrow? You'd inherit nothing. Lasair Gheug would have it all."

"I'm not worried about that," said the queen, but the Hen Wife could see that it was a lie.

"Give me seven sacks of meal, seven pounds of butter and seven sacks of fleece," said the Hen Wife, "and I'll tell you what to do."

"Very well," said the queen.

When the queen had fulfilled her side of the bargain, the Hen Wife came back. "I'll tell you what we'll do," she said to the queen. "We'll kill the king's best hound and say that Lasair Gheug did it. I'll put a spell on her so she can't tell."

They killed the hound and wiped its blood on Lasair Gheug's skirt. "You cannot tell of this to any baptised soul," said the Hen Wife, "though you stand on foot, though you be on horseback, though you be anywhere on the green earth."

When the king came home and found his hound dead, he roared out, "Who did this deed?"

"Your own daughter," said the queen. "Lasair Gheug."

"I don't believe it," said the king, and he shut himself in his great chamber.

The next morning the Hen Wife came to find the queen.

"What did the king do to Lasair Gheug?" she asked.

"Nothing," said the queen. "He didn't believe she killed the dog. Be off with you, you horrid old woman. I never wish to see you again."

"Now, now, now," said the Hen Wife. "I'll tell you what we'll do. We'll kill the king's finest horse and say that Lasair Gheug did it. She's still under my spell and so she can't tell."

They killed the horse and wiped its blood on Lasair Gheug's skirt.

When the king came home and found his fine

mare dead, he roared out, "Who did this deed?"

"Your daughter," said the queen. "Your precious Lasair Gheug."

"I don't believe it," said the king, and he slammed the door of his chamber.

Again the Hen Wife came to find the queen, and again the queen told her that the king had not believed the story. "I'm done with this," the queen said. "Leave me in peace."

"No, no, no," said the Hen Wife. "A little patience is all you need. We'll kill the king's fine bull – then he'll believe Lasair Gheug has done it. You'll see."

And so they killed the bull, but again the king refused to believe that Lasair Gheug was guilty.

"Tell him you're dying," said the Hen Wife to the queen. "That's the only thing left that will work."

And so the queen took to her bed, and her waiting women wept and lamented and told the king she was sure to die.

"Can nothing be done?" asked the king.

"Lasair Gheug is behind this illness," said the Hen Wife. "Bring your wife her heart, her liver and her little finger. Only then will she be well."

"Very well," said the king, and with a heavy heart

he went to find his daughter.

Lasair Gheug wished desperately to tell her father all that her stepmother and the Hen Wife had done, but whenever she opened her mouth to speak, the Hen Wife's spell bound her tongue as surely as if she were mute. Instead she looked the king straight in the eye, and he saw that her heart was good.

"Come," he said, "to the kitchen. The sandy-haired cook will help us."

In the kitchen the king told the sandy-haired cook what he needed, and the cook agreed to kill a suckling pig and cut out its heart and its liver. Then the king put Lasair Gheug on his horse, with a peck of silver and a peck of gold, and they rode until they came to a forest without edge or end. At nightfall they came to a house and the king bade Lasair Gheug climb down from the horse and go inside.

"I will leave this gold and silver with you, and my blessing," he said. "But I must ask you to do one terrible thing. May I cut off the tip of your finger? Only then will the queen believe you are truly gone. Only then will you be safe from the witch's meddling."

Lasair Gheug held out her hand and her father cut off the tip of her little finger.

"Does it hurt you very badly?" he asked, as Lasair

Gheug bound her hand in her apron.

"No," said Lasair Gheug, "for you did it, Father, and I know you would never seek to hurt me."

The king went home and gave the pig's liver and its heart and Lasair Gheug's own finger to the queen. The queen was well again in an instant. The king went to his own bed and lay deaf and blind to the world with grief at the loss of his hound, his mare, his fine bull and his beloved daughter.

Alone in the house in the forest, Lasair Gheug became afraid. She lit a fire and she found bread and cheese in a dresser for her dinner, but she had no idea what she would do come morning. She had a peck of silver and a peck of gold, but what use would those be in the forest? She lay down by the fire and tried not to cry with loneliness.

In the dark heart of the night, Lasair Gheug heard a scratching at the door and a mewling. She opened the door and saw six black cats and a white cat.

"I smell knight's blood, or king's blood," said the white cat. "Who are you, wounded and alone here in the forest, with the smell of royal blood about you?"

"I am the King of Ireland's daughter," Lasair Gheug told him. "And I'm hiding from my stepmother. She wishes me dead. I will give you all my gold and all my silver if you won't tell her where I am."

"Keep your gold and silver," said the grey cat. "Will you let us spend the night here in the house with you?"

"I will, and welcome," said Lasair Gheug.

When Lasair Gheug awoke in the morning, the cats had disappeared. Instead she found six knights asleep on the floor, around a handsome prince.

"Who are you?" she cried.

"I'm the son of the King of Lochlann," said the prince. "I was under a witch's spell but the spell has been broken by your kindness. I would like to repay your good deed, Lasair Gheug. Marry me and come with me, home to Lochlann."

Lasair Gheug's heart leaped with joy. Just the day before she had been lonely and afraid, sure that the queen would find her and kill her. Now she had a husband and a family, and a safe home across the sea. The only sadness in her heart was that her father would not know of her happiness. As she thought of him, a thought crossed her mind.

"I have one condition," she said. "I do not wish our children to be baptised."

"As you wish," said the Prince of Lochlann. He snapped his fingers, and they were at home in

Lochlann, where his parents wept with joy to see their son again, and immediately took Lasair Gheug to their hearts as a daughter, for she had broken the witch's curse. They held a great wedding feast and there was rejoicing through the land as every year for three blessed years, a son was born to Lasair Gheug and her prince.

Back home in Ireland, the queen went to a well in the palace gardens to fetch water to wash her face. There was a trout in this well that was magical, and the queen said, "Little trout, little trout, am I not the bonniest woman that ever lived in Ireland?"

"Indeed and indeed then you are not," said the trout. "Not as long as Lasair Gheug lives." It flicked its tail and flashed away, splashing the queen on the nose.

"If Lasair Gheug lives still," said the queen, "I will set a snare to trap her, and I will set a net to trap you!"

"You've tried that before," the trout called back, "and you'll never succeed. Mighty is the water I will swim in by nightfall."

Furious, the queen rushed back to her room and slammed the door. She called for the Hen Wife and shouted and roared at the witch for allowing her to believe that Lasair Gheug was dead.

"Calm yourself," said the Hen Wife. "I will put this right."

The Hen Wife gave the queen a box of gold closed tight with a key. They wrapped it in the king's banner and sent it to Lochlann. When Lasair Gheug opened the box, three hailstones flew out. One struck her in the forehead and one in either hand, and she fell down dead.

The prince was heartbroken by his wife's death. He had her body placed in a coffin of lead and kept it in her room in the palace. He visited her early and late, and every day he stayed longer than the day before. His parents could not bear to see him so bereft, and eventually they began to suggest that he should marry again for the children's sake. They found a kindly girl who came to the palace and cared for the three motherless boys as if they were her own. Gradually the prince began to smile again. But marry he would not, and he would not give up the key to Lasair Gheug's room.

Eventually the queen took pity on the girl who so wished to marry her son, and took her into the room where Lasair Gheug lay. "He cannot let her go," she said. "I'm sorry if we have raised your hopes for nothing."

The girl walked over to Lasair Gheug and peered at her closely. "How alive she looks," she said. "As though she were merely asleep." She leaned a little closer. "What's this on her face?" she asked, and picked up the little hailstone. "And look here – there are two more in her hands."

As soon as the girl had removed the hailstones, Lasair Gheug sat up and yawned as though she were waking from the most delicious nap. "Good morning, Mother," she said to the queen. "And who is this?"

The prince was mad with joy when he saw Lasair Gheug restored to life once more. He vowed that the girl should stay with them for the rest of her life, and that she would have fine clothes and jewels, minstrels and poets and anything that would bring her joy, for she had restored all of the love and laughter to their lives. She and Lasair Gheug became the best of friends and the queen felt that she was the luckiest of women, for now she had two daughters when before she had none.

Over in Ireland the queen went to the well on a fine May morning to wash her face in the waters.

"Little trout, little trout," said she, "am I not the

bonniest woman that ever lived in Ireland?"

"Indeed and indeed then you are not," said the trout. "Not as long as Lasair Gheug lives."

Quick as a flash, the queen grabbed at the trout, but the trout was faster and it dived away.

The queen ran to the king's room in a fury and banged on the door.

"Your daughter is still alive!" she yelled. "In Lochlann! Stir yourself, man! We must go and bring her home."

Lasair Gheug felt no joy in her heart when she saw her father's banners approaching. She sent her men out to bring home a wild boar.

"Do not slaughter it yet," she said. "Tie it well and bring it here to me."

The men thought Lasair Gheug was mad, but they brought the boar into the great hall and held it by ropes so that its head was still. Lasair Gheug climbed on to its back and summoned her maids to bring her three unbaptised children to her.

"I cannot tell this tale to anyone but you," she whispered to her children. "And you must tell my father. My stepmother and the Hen Wife killed his hound and his horse and his bull, and they said that I had done it. I did no such thing, but they bound me with a spell and I could not tell."

When she had told her story, the men let go of the boar, and the boar ran straight for Lasair Gheug's stepmother, and ran her through. Then the children told their father what had happened, and he told the King of Ireland, and the king said that he had long known that Lasair Gheug was as good of heart as his wife was evil. And Lasair Gheug told him how she had missed him and worried about him, and he apologized for the cutting of her finger and for casting her out.

"You wanted to keep me safe," she said, "and now I will charge you with keeping another girl safe, for she is as dear to me as anyone." And she brought out her friend to meet her father, and soon he asked her to go home to Ireland and be his queen.

The wedding lasted for a year and a day and was as full of mirth and merriment and joy as the hearts of Lasair Gheug and her prince.

Bold Girls

A SCOTTISH RIDDLE

How is a woman like an echo?

ANSWER
She always has the last word.

Across the world today, women and girls appear less often in films and television than men do. Books for children and young people are almost twice as likely to feature a male main character than a female one.

Scotland's folk and fairy tales are much better than modern films and books at featuring brave, bold girls and women as central characters. The Scottish fairy tale world is not entirely equal – more than half of wicked characters are women – but you will find some brilliant, determined female role models in the following stories to inspire you.

Molly Whuppie

Molly Whuppie is a story from the Lowlands of Scotland. It appears in Joseph Jacob's collection, and there is also a Gaelic version called "Maol a' Chliobain". This version uses Molly's Lowland name, but otherwise it is based on the Gaelic story.

It is related to the story of "Jack and the Beanstalk", although there is no beanstalk. Instead Molly faces a choice – less food with her mother's blessing, or more food without. Characters in Gaelic stories often face this choice.

It is very unusual for stories like this one to have girls as their central characters. Go, Molly Whuppie!

Once upon a time there lived three sisters – Sheena, Christina and Molly. The sisters' father had died and their mother was very poor. One day, she told them there was no food left in the house, aside from three bannocks.

Sheena looked at her feet and Christina began to cry. Molly frowned at them and then she smiled at her mother.

"There's only one thing to be done," she said. "We must go and seek our fortune. Me, and Sheena, and Christina."

"Us?" said Sheena, who wasn't used to doing very much at all. "Go and seek—"

"Our fortune?" said Christina. She was even lazier than Sheena. If she could have got away with it, she would have lain in bed all day while her mother brought her food and drinks.

"Yes," said Molly. "We're big bold girls, are we not? Of course we'll help our mother."

"Oh, Molly," said their mother. "Bless you."

Sheena and Christina weren't pleased, but when they saw how happy their mother was, they knew they couldn't very well refuse to go with their sister. They glared at Molly as they put on their coats and shoes and found a bag to fill with food for the journey.

"Take the bannocks," their mother said. She opened the cupboard and took out the bannocks.

"One of them is only small," said Sheena.

"VERY small," said Christina.

"That's true," said their mother, "but whoever takes the little bannock, she shall have my blessing too."

Sheena and Christina looked at her as though she were mad. Then they took the big bannocks. The smallest bannock was left for Molly.

"I'll take the small one with pleasure," said Molly happily. "For I would prefer my mother's blessing any day than a little more to eat."

Her mother kissed her. "My blessing on you, Molly," she said. "I don't know what I'd do without you."

"Stuff and nonsense," said Christina. "A blessing won't keep the hunger away." She turned to Molly. "Come on, then, Molly," she said. "If we have to go, we'd better go before it gets dark."

They set off and followed a little path up into the mountains. All the while Molly was singing and whistling and chatting cheerily. Her sisters didn't say much, only that their feet were sore or that they were getting tired.

"I wish," said Sheena at last, "that we'd never left home. This is a stupid plan."

"It is," said Christina. "We'd have found some money somehow."

"You're right, Christina," said Sheena. "Our mother could have taken in washing for people, or gone and worked for them as a cook."

"Indeed she could have!" said Christina. "You should have said that before we left, Sheena."

Molly was growing crosser and crosser as she listened to this, but she knew her sisters and she kept her temper to herself. "Who knows?" she said. "Maybe you'll meet a rich man to marry."

"Oh," said Sheena.

"Ah," said Christina.

"Yes," said Molly. "I think it's more than likely."

"But our dresses and our shoes will be ruined with dust from the road," Sheena complained. "What nobleman will look at us then?"

"You're right, Sheena," said Christina. "This *is* a stupid plan."

Christina pulled Sheena aside so that Molly couldn't hear them. "Molly's so cheerful all the time," she said. "What if the nobleman picks her to marry?"

Sheena was furious. "The little weasel!" she said.

"Stealing our husbands like that! She should be ashamed of herself!"

"Wouldn't it be better," Christina said, "if she wasn't with us at all?"

And so, the next time they passed a big rock by the road, the sisters leaped on Molly and they tied her to the rock.

"We'll be faster without you, Molly," Christina said. "But we'll come back for you. You won't get lost, because you're tied to this rock."

I see, thought Molly. *For while my sisters drag their feet and dawdle, it's me, Molly, who is slowing them down!*

"Aren't we nice sisters," said Sheena, "looking after you all the time?"

Sheena and Christina headed off up the road. Molly shook her head.

"Come back for me indeed," she said to herself. "I reckon I'll be waiting a while."

Molly couldn't do very much about it, though, and she was not the sort of girl to get worked up over a silly sister, and so she waited to see what would happen. A little while later she heard a whistle and then she saw someone coming along the path. It was an old man, with raggedy clothes and a grubby face.

"What's this?" the old man said. "A little girl tied to a rock? Who did this to you, poor creature?"

The old man had a knife and he cut the rope and let Molly go. And then he made a fire and boiled water for tea for the two of them. Molly took out her bannock and gave him half of it. She put the other half in her pocket.

"Are you not hungry?" the old man asked.

"Yes," said Molly, "but my mother gave me the bannock with her blessing, and I'd like to keep it a little while longer." Then she told him about her sisters and what they had done.

"Well," said the old man, "I had planned to go the other way today, but I took a notion to come along this path. Perhaps your mother's blessing put the idea in my head."

"Perhaps," said Molly.

They drank their tea and then Molly said she should go and find her sisters.

"Best of luck, Molly," the old man said. "Take this, and if they try the same thing again, you can get away." And he gave her a little knife.

Molly thanked him and put the knife in her pocket. Then she said goodbye to the old man and walked on up the road. Around evening she found her sisters sitting by the path arguing with one another.

"Look!" said Christina to Sheena. "Where did she come from?"

"Molly!" said Sheena. "We were just about to come and get you."

Molly let the lie pass, and smiled at her sisters instead. "Well, I saved you a little time, then."

Molly made them all tea and they settled down for the night.

In the morning the sisters began their complaining again.

"We've got no breakfast," said Sheena.

"Where are your bannocks?" asked Molly.

"We ate them last night," said Christina.

"Oh," said Molly.

"Have you not eaten yours?" asked Sheena.

"Yes, I have," said Molly. *If I say I haven't*, she thought, *they'll eat that too and I'll have nothing.*

They set off once again. They hadn't gone far when Molly heard Sheena and Christina whispering to one another.

"How do you think she got away?"

"Who knows? She won't manage it next time."

In a short while they came to a place where there

was a peat stack, and Sheena and Christina leaped on Molly and tied her to the stack.

"Wait there, Molly," said Christina. "We'll come back for you in the evening."

And off they went. Molly waited until they were out of sight before she took out the knife and cut the rope. Then she had a look about and she found some wild garlic and mushrooms she knew were good to eat. She made a little fire with a peat and cooked her breakfast. Then she had a nap before she set off in search of her sisters.

She found them sitting a little further along by the path arguing and complaining. When they saw Molly, Sheena frowned and Christina's mouth tightened into a little line.

When Molly woke the next morning, the knife was gone from her pocket. The bannock was still in her other pocket, because it had been under her as she slept.

This time, they tied Molly to a tree. They left her there and ran off. Molly put her hand in her pocket and took out the bannock. "Well," she said, "at least they left me that."

Molly couldn't do anything about her situation, and so she waited. She sat so still that the beasts and the birds and the beasties grew used to her. They came closer and Molly threw crumbs of bannock on the ground for them. The beasts and the birds and the beasties ate the crumbs, and then they crept up to Molly and chewed through the rope binding her to the tree.

"Thank you!" said Molly. "Thank you all!"

Molly scattered more crumbs on the ground and then ran up the road. She found her sisters lying on the ground a little way on, crying and moaning with hunger.

"How did you get away this time?" Sheena asked. "Little weasel."

"My mother's blessing," said Molly. "It saved me from my sisters' ill will."

"Will it save us from hunger?" asked Sheena.

"Perhaps," said Molly. "If you promise not to do anything so bad again."

"We promise," said Christina. "Anyway, it was Sheena."

"It was not!" said Sheena. "It was you! I'm sorry, Molly."

Molly shared the bannock between her sisters and went off to look for more to eat. A little way from the road, she saw smoke rising from the chimney of a house.

"Sheena! Christina!" she cried. "A house!"

The sisters knocked on the door of the house. It opened and a woman peered out.

"Be off with you, girls," the woman cried. "Go home. This is no place for you."

"Oh, please," said Sheena. "We're starving. We've had nothing but crumbs to eat for three days."

After a moment, the woman sighed and stepped back. They followed her in.

"Once you've eaten," she said, "you must go. My husband is a giant and he would eat three young girls if he knew you were here."

They sat at the table and the giant's wife gave them soup and bread. She told them the giant had stolen her from her father's house to look after his three daughters. They were out with their father.

When they had eaten, Molly stood and said that she and her sisters would go.

"But it's so warm here," said Sheena. "And we're so tired. Just five more minutes."

"No more minutes," said the giant's wife. "Go now." But no matter what she said, Sheena and Christina wouldn't listen.

"Oh, no," said the giant's wife. "You're too late. I hear my husband coming."

And then they all heard the terrible steps on the path outside. The door opened and in came the biggest and most horrid man they had ever seen, with a dead deer in his hands. Behind him came three girls. They looked even more horrid than their father. Each one held a dead swan, and their aprons were covered in blood. When they saw Molly and her sisters, they stopped so quickly that the one in the back bumped into the others.

"What have we here?" asked the giant.

"Poor, thin, hungry girls with no meat on their bones," his wife said, "and they're just leaving."

"Now, now, you mustn't leave," said the giant with a terrible smile. "We've brought dinner home with us. You must stay and eat." He turned and winked at his daughters.

They had no choice but to stay. The giant's wife cooked the meat and they sat at the great table. When they had eaten, the giant said that Molly and her sisters could stay there for the night. "I'll give you a present too," he said, and he gave them all a string of pearls. "Put them on, girls."

Sheena and Christina oohed and aahed. But Molly saw the giant wink at his daughters again when they put the necklaces on.

That night Molly and her sisters slept in the giant sisters' bed. Molly waited until the giant sisters were asleep, and then she took off her own and her sisters' necklaces and put them on the giants instead. Then she closed her eyes and pretended to sleep.

In the middle of the night, the giant crept across to the bed and fumbled around until he worked out which girls were wearing the pearls. He had a great club, and when he found each necklace, he used the club to hit the girl wearing it. When he had found the three strings of pearls and struck three heads, he crept back to his own bed.

Poor Molly was shaking with fear. She waited until she heard the giant's snores again, and then she woke her sisters and told them what had happened. They crept out of the house on their tiptoes and ran and ran until they could no longer see the house. They walked all night, and in the morning they came to a castle.

They knocked on the door of the castle and were taken inside. They told the servants about the giant, and the servants took them to the king and queen.

"Well, well, Molly Whuppie," said the king. "No one has ever bested that giant, but you did. A young girl. Well, well."

Then the queen told them that the giant had stolen almost everything precious from the castle over many years.

"Would you go back there, Molly?" she asked. "We would be very grateful. My son Alan would marry your sister Christina as thanks." Alan was the queen's oldest son.

"Wow!" said Christina. "Go on, Molly. Say you'll do it."

Molly agreed – not for Christina, but for the queen, who had looked so sad when she told them that the giant had stolen her mother's comb.

"It's a magic comb," said Donald, the queen's youngest son. "It makes the hair of anyone who uses it as strong as rope. That's how the giant ties up the animals he steals."

That night, after dark, Molly left the castle and returned to the giant's house. When she heard the giant and his wife snoring, she crept in and found the comb on a dresser by the bed. She was almost at the door with it when she tripped over a stool that landed with a clatter. Quick as a flash the giant was out of bed and after her. Molly ran at full tilt until she could run no more. There was a river before her and it was flowing too fast for her to swim across.

Just as she heard the giant's steps behind her, Molly remembered what Donald had said about the comb. She pulled it through her own hair, and it became as strong as a rope. She pulled out a strand and tied it across the river like a bridge. She ran across it to the other side just as the giant appeared on the opposite bank. He tried to climb on the hair, but his feet were too big.

"Curse you, Molly Whuppie!" the giant roared. "You've stolen my comb! Don't you come back here again or I'll rip you limb from limb!"

Molly ran back to the castle and gave the comb to the queen. The queen was overjoyed and set about arranging the marriage between Christina and Alan.

The night before the wedding, Sheena came to find Molly.

"I know I wasn't always very nice to you, Molly," she said. "I'm sorry for it, for you are a loving sister."

Molly understood from this that Sheena had fallen in love with Ronald, Alan and Donald's brother, and wished to marry him.

"Very well," she sighed. "What do I have to get this time?"

Donald explained to Molly that the golden lamp the giant had stolen from his father was a magic lamp. It would only shine for the person who lifted it. That was how the giant stole animals in the darkness.

That night, after dark, Molly left the castle and returned again to the giant's house. She crept in and found the lamp on the dresser. She crept towards the door, but as she opened it the giant's dog woke up and began to bark. The giant leaped out of bed and ran after Molly. Molly ran for her life to the river, where the lamp revealed the bridge of one hair and she ran across.

The giant could see nothing in the dark. "Curse you, Molly Whuppie!" he roared. "You've stolen my lamp! Don't you come back here again or I'll rip you limb from limb!"

Molly went back to the castle and the king was overjoyed to have his lamp back. Sheena's wedding to Ronald and Christina's wedding to Alan took place that very day. At the end of the evening, the king and queen came to find Molly.

"We are in your debt, Molly Whuppie," the queen said. "And we have grown very fond of you. As has Donald. He would like to marry you."

"Oh," said Molly, and her cheeks flamed red. "I would like that too."

"There's one thing. . ." said the king. "Donald, you see, is under a spell. He can only marry with a gold ring stolen by—"

"Yes, yes," Molly sighed. "I understand."

Donald told Molly about the ring. It was a magic one, that could only be worn by a brave girl with a pure heart.

"That's you, Molly," he said.

Molly's cheeked flamed even redder.

The next night, after dark, Molly left the castle and returned once more to the giant's house. There were no snores or other noises and she decided the giant and his wife were not at home. She crept in and found the ring on the dresser. She turned to leave but the giant was waiting behind the door. He grabbed Molly and stuffed her in a sack.

"Well, Molly Whuppie," he said, "I have you now." He called out to his wife. "Morag? Morag? What will I do with this little weasel?"

"I don't know," said his wife, and she began to cry at the thought of all of the dreadful things her awful husband might do to Molly Whuppie.

"I'll tell you what I'd do if I were you," said Molly from the sack, thinking as quickly as she could. "I'd hang this sack from a nail on the wall. Then I'd go right into the heart of the forest and find the biggest, strongest stick I could. Then I'd come home and beat the sack and beat the sack until Molly Whuppie was dead and could steal from me no longer."

"Good idea!" shouted the giant. He hung the sack on the wall and ran out of the house.

Molly thanked her lucky stars that the giant was every bit as stupid as she had hoped. "Quick!" she shouted to the giant's wife. "Get me out!"

The giant's wife let Molly out of the sack. They filled it with peat and hung it back on the wall. Then they ran out of the house to the river and crossed the bridge of one hair. When they reached the other side, Molly cut the hair and the bridge fell into the water.

When the giant got home again with his stick, he beat the sack and beat the sack and shouted, "Take that, Molly Whuppie!" and, "I'll show you," and, "Steal my precious things, would you?" By the time he realized that Molly and his wife were gone, they had already reached the castle.

Molly married Donald, who knew how lucky he was to have found a wife who was bold and pure of heart.

The queen gave the giant's wife a job as a cook.

Molly's mother came to look after her grandchildren.

And Sheena and Christina were as silly, mean and conceited as ever.

The Old Man with the Grain of Barley

All across the world there are tales of tricksters – crafty characters who use cunning to get food, steal precious possessions or generally cause mischief. Often trickster tales have animal characters such as foxes. In this Gaelic story all the characters are human, but the trickster isn't as tricky as he thinks!

Once upon a time there lived an old man who had no wealth in the world but his wits. One fine morning, this old man said to himself that it was high time he went off to seek his fortune. He set out before the dew was off the grass, and he was barely past his own gate when he spotted a grain of barley in a sandy hollow by the side of the road.

"Ah ha!" he chuckled to himself. "I've found my fortune, or the means of making it at least. That didn't take very long at all, and I'll be rich soon with very little need to trouble myself."

The old man picked up the grain of barley and walked on down the road.

In a little while the old man reached a house in a field by the road. He knocked on the door and the people welcomed him in.

"I'm off to seek my fortune," the wily old man told them. "Would you be so good as to mind this grain of barley for me until I return in a month and a day? It's very precious to me, for I have nothing else in the world."

If the woman of the house thought the request a little odd, she didn't say so. Instead she smiled kindly. "Of course we will."

The old man went off, but instead of walking onwards, he turned back to his own home to take things nice and easy.

In a month and a day, the old man returned to the house. When the woman saw him at the door, she wrung her hands.

"I've come back to fetch my grain of barley," said the old man.

"Oh, my," said the woman. "Our brown hen ate it!"

The old man suppressed a smile of glee. "If that's true," he said, "I'll have to take the hen, for it ate my grain of barley, the only thing I had in the world. It's only fair."

The woman was so embarrassed that she immediately agreed. The old man tucked the brown hen under his arm and walked off down the road. In a little while he reached another house where he knocked and was made welcome.

"I'm off to seek my fortune," said the old man. "Would you be so good as to mind this hen for me until I return in a month and a day? It's very precious to me, for I have nothing else in the world."

"Of course we will," said the man of the house happily. "We'll enjoy the eggs."

All the way home the old man laughed at his cleverness. For a month and a day he did nothing but gloat at the thought of how his fortune would increase. When the time was over, he returned.

"I've come back to fetch my brown hen," said the old man.

"Oh dear," said the man. "There was a terrible accident. Our speckled cow trampled the hen!"

"If that's the case," said the old man, "I'll have to take the cow, for it killed my hen, the only thing I had in the world. It's only fair."

The man of the house looked terribly guilty and in the end he agreed. The old man took hold of the cow's halter and he set off down the road. At the next house he reached, he knocked and the people took him in.

"I'm off to seek my fortune," said the old man. "Would you be so good as to mind this cow for me until I return in a month and a day? It's very precious to me, for I have nothing else in the world."

"Of course we will," said the couple in the house.

The old man went home and waited a month and a day, and then he returned.

"I've come back to fetch my speckled cow," said the old man.

The couple looked at one another sadly. "There was a terrible accident," the man said. "Our youngest daughter took the cow to the loch, and the cow fell in and drowned!"

This is better than I ever imagined! thought the old man. *Now I will have a wife to keep house for me and raise my hens and grow my cabbages and I will never have to lift a finger again!* "If that's what happened," he said, making sure his face was solemn, "I'll have to take the girl, for she drowned my cow, the only thing I had in the world. It's only fair."

The old man took out a sack and signalled to the girl to climb in.

The couple were very embarrassed, but not so embarrassed as to agree that a daughter was a fair exchange for a cow. And so, when the old man asked for something to tie his sack, the woman told him where to find a piece of heather rope in the byre.

As soon as the old man had gone outside, she handed her daughter a pair of scissors. "Don't let on that you have these," she said, "but get away as fast as you can and run back home."

As soon as the old man tied up the sack, the girl began to lament and wail. He said not a word, but hoisted the sack over his shoulder and walked on down the road. But the day was warm, the sack was heavy, and the girl was loud. Before he had gone very far at all the old man felt the need to sit down and rest. In a few moments, he was fast asleep in the sun.

The girl had a clever mind and a determined spirit, and as soon as she realized her captor had gone quiet, she stopped wailing and listened. When she heard snoring, she cut a small slit in the sack with the scissors, slid her hand out and untied the knot in the rope. Then she filled the sack with stones, tied it up tight and ran like the wind for home.

As afternoon turned to evening, an ant walked across the old man's nose and he woke with a start.

"Well, well," he said to the sack, "at least you've quietened down now." He stood up and stretched, and then he picked up the sack and headed on down the road. He didn't stop until dusk. He put the sack down in a dip by the road and opened it.

"Well, well," the old man said to the stones. "No wonder you didn't have a lot to say."

In the morning, the old man left the sack and the stones in the grass and he walked on down the road. Before he had gone very far at all, he spotted a grain of barley in the grass.

"Ah ha!" said he. "Here's my new fortune. Let's see what we can do with this."

He picked up the grain of barley and walked on down the road.

The Counting Out of Fionn and Dubhan's Men

This is an unusual story from Gaelic tradition – it's based on a famous mathematical puzzle.

The puzzle starts with fifteen black and fifteen white pieces (you can use draughts or chess pieces or stones). The challenge is to lay the pieces out in a circle so that you can take away all the stones of one colour by counting the same number round the circle every time and taking those stones away.

The riddle is very old and appears under many names, such as "Ludus Sancti Petri" or "The Josephus Problem".

In this story, it is linked with the legendary hero Fionn MacCumhaill.

The great warlords Fionn MacCumhaill and Dubhan were as different as two men could be. Fionn was tall and broad, and Dubhan was short and stocky. Dubhan's hair was as black as coal and Fionn's was as yellow as gold. Dubhan's men wore dark leather armour, and Fionn's bright metal that shone like the sun. The two men were sworn enemies, but Dubhan's daughter had a secret fondness for Fionn. His exploits were heroic, and he fought fairly every time. Dubhan was much more likely to trick and swindle and cheat his way to what he wanted, and secretly she thought that her father was not an honourable man.

One day it happened that Fionn and Dubhan were aboard a ship with fourteen men each as escort. Dubhan's daughter was also on board. A dreadful storm blew up and it seemed that the ship would be lost.

Dubhan said to Fionn that they should lighten the load of the boat by half. "It's not far to shore," said he, "and the men won't break when they wash up on shore like the boat will. If they take their chances in the water, we might yet save the boat."

"Fine," said Fionn. "Your men should jump."

"No," said Dubhan. "It was my idea. *Your* men should take their chances."

After that, it seemed they could go no further.

Neither warlord was willing to lose his own men, for fear that the other would attack.

"I know what to do," said Dubhan's daughter. "I'll seat the men in a circle around me, and count out each ninth man. That way it will be fair. Both of you will take your own places in the circle, Father and Fionn."

Immediately Dubhan agreed, for of course he trusted his daughter to deal with them fairly. Reluctantly Fionn agreed too, for how could anyone cheat with such a complex count? Surely Dubhan's daughter's method would select an equal number of Fionn and Dubhan's men.

Dubhan's daughter sat the men in a circle sun-wise with a rhyme.

"Four of Fionn's men first I'll ask
to sit as I begin my task.
Five black warriors, sit before me
the best of Dubhan's company.

Two men more then from MacCumhaill
Followed up with one from Dubhan.
Three from Fionn to follow on
one from Dubhan, come along.

Fionn MacCumhaill, join you in,
two black fellows to follow him.
Two more heroes on their left hand
of Fionn MacCumhnaill's great war-band.

Next, brave Dubhan, you'll sit grand
With one black man on either hand.
Two from Dubhan follow one from
MacCumhaill,
Two from Fionn and one from Dubhan."

When all of the men were seated at last, Dubhan's daughter began to count every ninth man out.

"Aon, dhà, trì, ceithir, còig, sia, seachd, ochd, NAOI."

"Aon, dhà, trì, ceithir, còig, sia, seachd, ochd, NAOI."

"Aon, dhà, trì, ceithir, còig, sia, seachd, ochd, NAOI."

But every ninth man was one of her father's!

By the time Dubhan's daughter had finished her counting, every last one of Dubhan's men was swimming for his life in the roiling sea. The only black-armoured warrior left onboard was Dubhan.

His daughter took him by the arm to pull him to the side, but Fionn stopped her. For all Dubhan's tricks and cheating, Fionn decided that he would play fair, and he saved Dubhan a soaking.

They saved the boat, and reached shore safely.

How well do you think Dubhan and his daughter got on after that day?

This is how the pieces should be laid out, following the rhyme. Start counting at one, and take away every ninth piece. Start counting again at the next piece. In the end you should have only white counters left.

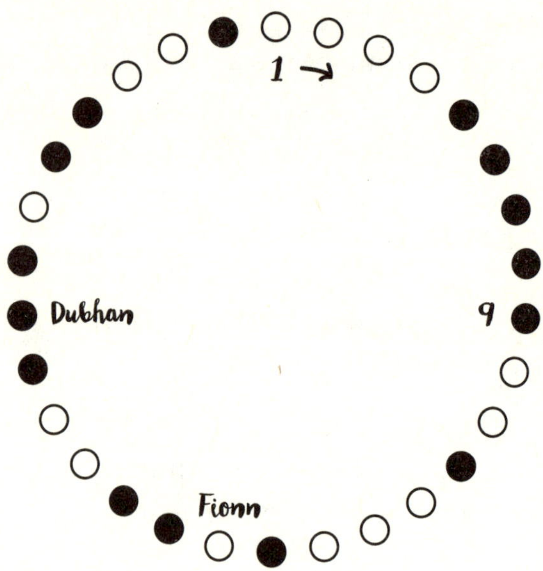

The Tale of the Hoodie Crow

This is a strange Gaelic wonder-tale from the West Highlands with many magical ingredients you will recognize – a bewitched man, a brave girl, children whisked away by magic, and a seemingly impossible task. When the story was written down by John Francis Campbell in the 1800s, the characters had no names, but they have been given them here. Màiri is the Gaelic for Mary, and it is pronounced Ma-ree. Eilidh is the Gaelic for Helen, and it is pronounced Ailee. Iseabail is the Gaelic for Isobel, and it is pronounced Ishabel. The story involves a wedding which is celebrated with a feast and games – a little like Highland games, with feats of strength, races, dancing and music.

Once upon a time there lived a farmer who had three daughters: Màiri, and Eilidh, and Iseabail. One day the girls were washing their clothes on the banks of a river, when a hoodie crow flew down and landed beside them.

The hoodie spoke to the eldest girl, Màiri.

"Am pòs thu mi?" he said. *Will you marry me?*

Màiri screeched in horror. "No, I will not, you insolent creature! An ugly brute is the hoodie."

The next day the hoodie returned while they were milking the cows.

"Am pòs thu mi?" he said to Eilidh, the second sister. *Will you marry me?*

Eilidh recoiled at the thought. "No, I will not, you insolent creature! An ugly brute is the hoodie. And wormy too!"

The hoodie flew off, but the next day he returned again while they were waulking the new tweed in the sunshine, stretching it and pounding it to make it strong and tight. He landed by the youngest daughter, Iseabail, and waited until she had finished her song.

"Am pòs thu mi?" he said. *Will you marry me?*

"I will," said Iseabail. "A pretty creature is the hoodie."

The next day they were married.

"I am bewitched," the hoodie told his new wife, "and I must be a crow by day or by night. Would you rather I was a man by day, and a crow by night, or a crow by day and a man by night?"

"I would rather you were a man all the time," said Iseabail, "but since you cannot be, I choose that you be a crow by night and a man by day."

It was daytime then, and as soon as Iseabail spoke, the hoodie turned into a fine fellow. But he turned back to a crow that night, and every night thereafter.

A few days after the wedding, the hoodie took Iseabail home to his own house. They lived there very happily, and after three quarters of a year had passed, they had a son. The night the child was born, the finest and most magical music was heard outside, and all across the land the people fell into an enchanted sleep. When they woke in the morning, Iseabail and the hoodie's child was gone, and although they searched and searched, they could not find hide nor hair of him.

Three more quarters passed, and a second son was born. This time they stood watch over him that first night, but the music came as it had come before. They all slept, and the child disappeared. A third time this happened, and Iseabail and the hoodie did not know what to do for sorrow. They sent for her father, and he said their house must be cursed like the hoodie himself.

"Come back to my house," Iseabail's father said. "I will ride ahead and you can follow after. You must take everything from this place and not leave anything behind, lest the curse hold you still."

And so they set out for Iseabail's father's house, but on the way Iseabail asked to turn back, for she realized she had forgotten her coarse comb. As soon as she spoke, the coach crumbled to ash beneath them and they fell on the road. Although it was broad daylight, Iseabail's husband turned once more into a hoodie, and he flew away, it seemed in fear.

Iseabail set out to follow, but the hoodie was swift on the wing and she could not catch up. If he was at the top of a hill, she was at the bottom. When she reached the top, he would be in the hollow below.

"He does not know me," she wept, and her heart felt as though it would break.

When night came, Iseabail had no place to rest her head, and so she walked on until at last she came to a house. There was kindly woman there and a toddling little boy, and Iseabail felt her heart yearn for the child, who was the same age as her own first, lost boy would have been.

"Come in and rest," said the woman. "I know your pain and your quest. The hoodie has been to this house and he just left. Sleep now, and you can follow him again tomorrow."

Iseabail slept and the next day the woman fed her and gave her water to wash and bid her good luck. Then Iseabail left to look for the hoodie once again. She saw him on a hill a little way off, but by the time she had climbed to the top of that hill he was in a hollow at the bottom. When she reached the hollow, he was on the brow of the next hill.

Again she found rest in a house where a woman lived alone with a yearling baby, and Iseabail yearned and yearned for the child, so like the second son she had lost. The next day passed in the same way, following the hoodie and taking shelter in another house by night. That woman had a tiny baby and Iseabail yearned and yearned for him too.

"Your hoodie husband has not come here yet," said this woman, "but I know he will. If you can stay awake and catch hold of him, you will lift the forgetting spell and have him back."

Iseabail tried and tried to stay awake, but she

was so weary from walking, and from the sorrow of losing her husband and her children, and the house was so warm, and in the end she fell asleep.

In the dark of the night something fell on to Iseabail's face and woke her up. It was her husband's gold ring, dropped by the hoodie in flight. She sat up and did her best to seize him, but all she caught was one feather from his wing before he flew away.

In the morning, Iseabail asked the housewife if she knew where the hoodie had gone.

"Over the hill of poison," the housewife said. "You know he is cursed. He has forgotten all he knew as a mortal man, and on this side of the hill he is all hoodie now. If you could follow him, you could help him remember, but you cannot. No mortal foot may walk over that hill."

"Surely there's a way," Iseabail said.

"You could go if you were shod with iron," said the housewife. "If you found a smith and learned to make horseshoes to fit your own hands and feet, then you could cross the hill."

And so Iseabail found the nearest smith and begged to be apprenticed to him, and in time she learned to heat the iron and hammer it to make shoes for horses' hooves. Then she made shoes for her own hands and her own feet, and when they were ready she put them on and went to the hill of poison. She walked across the hill, and on the other side she came to a town in a land she did not know.

The place was in merry uproar, for there was to be a great wedding that afternoon between the daughter of a nobleman and a magical creature who was a mortal man by day and a hoodie crow by night. The marriage was to be celebrated by games and feasting, and that morning before the ceremony there was to be a great race.

Iseabail's heart felt as though it was breaking anew in her breast when she heard that her husband had truly forgotten her and planned to marry another. The only glimmer of hope she had was that he could once again turn into a mortal man by day. She clung on to that thought, lifted her chin and set out for the nobleman's house where the wedding was to take place.

When Iseabail arrived she found the house almost deserted, for everyone had gone to the race. The only person in the house was a cook who was not best pleased, for he had to stay behind and prepare the midday meal while everyone else was out enjoying themselves. Iseabail said that she would prepare the food and let him go to see the race. Delighted, he agreed and ran off without a backward glance.

When the company returned in high spirits, Iseabail had soup and bannocks ready. When she saw her husband take his place at the table, she dropped his gold ring and his feather in a bowl of soup and asked the cook to place that bowl before the groom. The hoodie spooned up the ring, and then the feather, and a frown settled on his brow.

"Who made this soup?" asked the hoodie.

"What does it matter?" said the nobleman. "We need to make haste to the church for the marriage."

"I will make no marriage," said the hoodie. "Until I know who made this soup. These things mean something to me, but I know not what."

They brought up the cook and questioned him, and he confessed that he had gone to the race and instead the meal had been cooked by a girl who had come to the house that day. Then they sent for Iseabail. When he saw her, sunshine flooded the hoodie's face.

"This is my married wife," he said. "I was cursed to forget her, but she has taken the spell from me. She has crossed the hill of poison and lifted my forgetting from me." And he took Iseabail in his arms and they wept with joy and relief.

Iseabail and the hoodie bid farewell to the people of the house. The nobleman's daughter was upset, but her father consoled her with the thought that she might find a man who was mortal all the time instead of half of it.

Then Iseabail and the hoodie crossed the hill of poison hand in hand, and at the top Iseabail threw her horseshoes behind her to close the door to that other place. Then they walked to the last house where she had spent the night. The three housewives who had cared for Iseabail were waiting outside with the children in their arms and smiles on their faces.

"Sisters!" the hoodie said. "It has been many years since I last saw you."

"Indeed it has not, brother," said the third housewife, "for your wife spent a night in this house not many months since, and you were here in hoodie form. You were under a spell of forgetting and you fled from your wife. This is your youngest son, who was spirited away to me by the curse that befell you. I have cared for him with all the love I bear for you."

"This is your second son," said the second housewife. "You came to my house too, but the spell meant that you did not know me, and you did not wait for your wife."

"Here is your eldest boy," said the first housewife. "And now the curse is lifted from you entirely, because your wife who was destined to forget you would not forsake you, and she crossed the hill of poison for your sake. Never will you be a hoodie again, but a mortal man always."

Now Iseabail and the hoodie had their arms full of children and a circle of sisters and a bright future to look forward to, although they could not yet look ahead because their eyes were blurred with tears of joy and they were content just to gaze on one another's faces. They took their sons home the very next day and lived there together for many happy years.

The Fairies

A Scottish riddle

What can you keep when you give it?

Answer
A promise.

In stories from the Gaelic-speaking part of Scotland, the fairies cannot fly and they are not kind. These "little people" live under the earth in fairy hills or *sìthein* ("shee-en") and steal mortal women and babies away to live with them as servants and slaves. They enjoy a trick or a riddle and have a particular love of music, which means that they are always happy to steal musicians away for entertainment.

In other areas of Scotland, fairies are described as elf-like magical creatures ruled by a king and queen.

This otherworldly "Seelie Court" can cross into our world at Halloween, and peril faces mortals who meet them.

The Bagpipers of Bornish

This is a Gaelic story from the Hebridean island of South Uist, where a great many traditions were carried through the centuries by storytellers, pipers and other musicians.

Once upon a time there lived three brothers in the village of Bornish in South Uist. The elder two were renowned from one end of the island to the other, for the gift of piping filled them from their heads to their toes. Whenever there was a dance or a *cèilidh*, a wedding or a funeral, those boys were in great demand. Their youngest brother did not have the gift of music, and it grieved him sore.

One day, the two piping brothers set off for a wedding in the south of the island, leaving the youngest at home to tend the animals. He took the cattle out to graze on the slopes of a hill, far from the village. The grass grew green and lush there, but people avoided it because they said it was a *sìthean*, a fairy hill. The fairies might steal the goodness from the milk of cattle grazing there, and if the hill ever opened and a mortal went inside, they might never return home.

The boy from Bornish had heard tales of the fairies since he was in his cradle, but he was not afraid. After all, he thought bitterly, didn't they say the fairies mostly stole away musicians? He had no music in his soul at all.

While the cattle grazed, the boy dozed for a while in the midday sun. When he woke a mist had descended and he could not see where the cows had gone. Pulling his jacket tight about him, he got up. He had taken no more than two steps when he stopped short. A door had opened in the hill.

The boy knew what it meant to enter a *sìthean* – if he went in, he might never come out again. He thought for a moment, and then took out the knife that he always carried. It was made of iron, and somewhere in his memory was an idea that iron was sacred, offering protection against the little people. He stuck the knife in the door so that it could not close, took a deep breath, and stepped inside.

Inside the *sìthean* was a long, low room. The room was warm and smoky, lit only by a peat fire in the middle of the floor, and it took some moments for the boy's eyes to grow accustomed to the dim. When at last they did, he saw an old man sitting on a bench by the fire. He looked quite like a normal man, only smaller and more wizened, as though he were older than anyone who had ever lived.

"Come in," said the fairy man, "and sit by the fire. You're a bold boy to enter the *sìthean*. What do you want from me?"

"I don't want anything," said the boy, startled, but he sat down beside the old man on the bench.

"Everyone wants something," said the old man, and he drew on a smelly pipe that he had.

The boy thought for a moment. "There's only one thing I don't have," he said, "but it's not a thing anyone can give me."

"Tell me," said the fairy. "Although I think I already know."

And so the boy told the fairy the dearest dream in his heart – that he could have the gift of piping like his brothers, and golden notes could pour from his fingers to lift the soul of anyone who listened.

"I can give you that gift," said the fairy. "But you must give me something in return."

At that the boy was nervous. He had heard that the fairies traded children or happiness for their gifts. His worry must have showed in his face, for the old man gave a cackling laugh.

"I don't ask anything you can't keep when you give it," said the old man. "And that's your word. I ask you to give your word that you will never let on to anyone that you ever met me, no matter what happens or where we might meet again."

The boy grinned with relief. "I can give you that," he said. "And can you really give me the gift of piping in return?" It seemed too good to believe.

The fairy threw away his pipe and reached for the boy's hands. "Thread your fingers through my fingers," he said, "and put your mouth against mine." The boy did as he was asked, and he felt his soul fill up with the gift of piping.

"Be off with you," the old man said, and he picked up his pipe again. "Never come back to this place, and never forget what you've promised."

The boy ran to the door of the *sìthean*. On the other side he pulled out his knife and the door melted back into the hill. The mist had gone now and the boy found the cattle grazing contentedly as if no time had passed at all.

Back at the house, the boy was desperate to try out his new skill. He cast a longing glance at his father's pipes hanging on the wall, but he knew that they were precious and his brothers only played them on the most special of occasions. And so he found another set of bagpipes that his brothers had mended for a neighbour. These pipes were plainer, without the silver mounts or fine tassels of his father's, but they would do. He settled the bag under his arm and the drones against his shoulder, placed his fingers on the chanter and the blow-pipe in his mouth. He closed his eyes, blew up the bag and began to play.

The music was sublime. The tunes flowed out of him in an endless stream, jigs, strathspeys, reels and marches, laments and slow airs and all the parts of the *pibrochs*, the great music of the Highland bagpipe. He played all night and into the morning, and then he played on till noon.

When the elder brothers returned from the wedding they had no idea what to make of the music pouring from the house. No one in the island could play so finely, apart from them – no, not even them. They ran inside, eager to meet this travelling master, whoever he might turn out to be. They stopped short when they saw that the music flowed from their own brother.

The eldest brother listened in silence for a few tunes more, and then he lifted his father's pipes from the wall.

"You should play these, brother," he said, with tears in his eyes. "For these are the finest pipes in the island by far, and you are the finest piper."

The boy wiped tears of pride from his own eyes and took his father's pipes in his arms. He blew them up and tuned them, and began to play. Soon his brothers had fetched their own pipes and played with him, in perfect harmony.

The boy's fame travelled far and wide. He played at weddings and funerals, dances and *cèilidhs*, to welcome boats to harbour and to send them safely on their way again. Day and night he played, and although it did not seem possible, he grew better and better with each week that passed. His brothers took their turn now to mind the cattle and the sheep, and they carried on mending bagpipes for the neighbours. Sometimes they all played together, but the elder two were shy in the face of their youngest brother's talent, and they always waited for him to invite them.

Years passed, and the boy married and had children of his own. He had almost forgotten the old man in the fairy hill, but as he taught his own children to play the pipes, he remembered him and wished he could say thank you for the great gift the man had given him.

One day around this time, an old woman died who had been a neighbour of the boy's parents, and the family asked the three brothers to walk ahead of her on her last journey to her eternal home. They tuned their pipes and stepped slowly ahead of the coffin on the long road to the grave.

Suddenly, a familiar face caught the boy's

eye – lined and wizened, older you might say than any mortal ever to live on the earth. The boy's heart leaped with joy, for he knew his fairy helper in an instant, and now he could tell him how grateful he was for the gift that had made his life complete. His brothers played on while he ran to the side of the road and grasped the fairy by the hand.

The fairy lifted his eyes to the boy's face, and they were as cold as stone. He turned away without a word and the boy watched him go with a pain in his heart that he could not name.

Only then did the boy remember the promise that he had given and broken without a moment's thought. He felt all the music in his soul turn to ashes, and his hands turn to lead by his sides. His father's fine bagpipes felt light all of a sudden, and turning his head he saw that all he held was a scrap of goatskin and a handful of rushes.

The boy never played again, and he never heard the sweet voice of the pipes without a pang of regret that he had not remembered how important it was to keep his word.

The Ropes of Sand

Stories about otherworldly helpers are common across the world. One famous version is "The Elves and the Shoemaker", a story collected in Germany by the Brothers Grimm. This is a Scottish Gaelic story, and in it a group of villagers struggle to be rid of their helpers. Historically Scotland has a strong work ethic, and perhaps this comes across in this story!

Once upon a time, and it was not so very long ago, most people lived close to the land and worked it with the toil of their hands. They knew every hillock and every hollow, every burn and every lochan, and every place where a well sang with pure, clean water.

Back then people understood that they did not have sole dominion over the land. They shared it with the wild birds and the animals. They shared it with the ghosts of those who had gone before. And they shared it with the fairies, the little people who dwelled below the ground.

The fairies were not easy neighbours. They were known to foretell deaths, and to steal away infants and leave changelings in their place to wither and sicken. They stole the goodness from milk, and sometimes they took the whole herd of cattle, and a dairymaid too for good measure.

In order to save themselves and their dear ones from the unknown fate of those who vanished into a fairy hill, people followed a set of rules, for in some things the fairies played fair.

When a child was born, its first gift would be a silver coin or an iron nail placed in its cradle, to keep the fairies away. No one would ever knowingly stray near a fairy hill, and a handful of oatmeal in the pocket protected those who might do so unawares. Marsh marigolds hung near a byre would protect the living beasts within, and a rowan tree by the gate watched over the inhabitants of a house. If a farm wife or dairymaid went to a wedding and knew she would be late to the milking the next day, she might lay iron nails or silver pins around her sleeping cows to shield them from the fairies and their milking stools.

The fairies were not all bad, and sometimes they gave as well as took. The trouble then was that it was hard to stop the fairies giving, as the people of one little settlement discovered to their cost.

This place was so tiny that you would struggle to find it on a map. No more than a dozen families lived there, and the hard work was shared evenly among them. Many hands made light work of launching a boat, and the men of the village worked together well as a fishing crew, with their nets and lines and creels. They hunted for seals and seabirds, bringing home eggs and meat, feathers for pillows, skins to keep out the cold and oil to burn in the lamps on a winter's night.

Men and women worked the land together,

turning the soil by hand and dragging great loads of seaweed from the shore to spread out upon it and make it good, so that their oats and barley and kale grew strong and green. At harvest time they toiled, scything and sheaving and stacking. They worked in teams to mend the thatches and cut the dark slabs of peat that would keep their houses cosy through the cold winter and cook their meals the whole year round. They tended the animals, milking the cows and the goats, churning the butter and pressing the cheeses. The men sheared the sheep and the women combed and carded and spun the wool, wove it into cloth and waulked it tight and strong around the great waulking board in the summer sun, with songs and merriment, while the men wove heather ropes and mended the creels, nets and harnesses.

When the work was done in the evenings the village came together to visit and worship. They sang and played pipes and fiddle, told stories to one another, prayed together, minded children, tended the sick, delivered babies and laid out the dead.

Life in this little place was not easy, though neither was it hard, and most of the inhabitants would have been content to go on for ever in that way. But there was one young man among them who had no love for the place. Alone of all his neighbours, he found no happiness in the warmth of toil. He hated the long hours out of doors and wished only to lie upon his bed and dream of faraway lands, doze, or while the hours away with a game of dice or knucklebones.

This young man's parents chased him and chivvied him, but still he dragged his feet and looked for any excuse to lag behind so that he could slip away from the peat-cutting or the fishing. Finally they shouted at him that he was a lazy, good-for-nothing son.

"I hate it here," the boy roared back. "I hate the stinking fish and smelly seaweed and filthy peat! I wish I never had another day's work to do in this place!"

Then he grabbed his blanket and ran off to sleep among the cows in the byre.

Next morning, the village stirred early as usual. It was to be a fishing day and the men had much to do to ready the boat. The women had their usual routine to follow – milking the cows and fetching the water, building up the fire and putting the porridge on.

Imagine the women's surprise when they found their peat fires glowing and the porridge steaming in the pot! Outside the cattle were cropping contentedly, their fetters put aside and the frothy, fresh milk ready and waiting in the wooden buckets. The milking stools were stowed away, there was good golden butter in the churn and sharp white cheese in the press. The byre was swept as clean as a new pin and there was fresh bedding raked out for the animals.

Dazed, the women fed their husbands and followed them to the shore, ready to launch the boat. They shook their heads and rubbed their eyes in wonder, for they were met by an enormous catch already on shore, neatly landed, gutted, salted and packed away. The nets were mended and folded and the boat tied up safely on the shore. A fire burned in a ring of rocks, and a mouth-watering smell came to them of fish fried in butter, in a crust of oatmeal.

The people sat in a dazed silence until the smell overcame them, and then they fell upon the food and ate and ate until they were full. Then they wandered back to their fields. All the work was done there too, and greater progress had been made than they could have hoped to achieve in several weeks.

"The fairies," someone said. "It must have been the fairies."

The people had no idea what to do, for leisure time was alien to them. In the end they fetched their fiddles and their pipes, a metal jaws-harp and a squeezebox, and they sat around the fire in the house of the eldest couple of all and sang and played. Someone found a precious bottle of whisky and they all drank a solemn toast to their fairy helpers.

A shooting star crossed the sky as the villagers left the *cèilidh* house and made their way to their beds. They looked about them but there was no sign of life beyond the smoke rising from their chimneys and the sigh of the sea nearby.

"That was a good day," someone said. "I'll always remember it."

They blessed one another, said their prayers and went to bed, sure that the next day things would be back to normal. But once more, they woke to find the chores were done. Linen shifts and shirts were washed snow white and woollen cloaks were beaten clean. Floors were swept and old coverings on the windows were replaced with clean new cloth, freshly oiled and tightly tied. Fires were glowing, porridge was cooking, there was cheese and milk, honey and oatcakes, a full catch of fish by the shore and a pile of sea birds, plucked and gutted and packed in barrels with salt, enough to last the winter and more.

The lazy young man did not get out of his bed that day. He lay on his blankets and dreamed, delighted with all the ease and bounty he had wished on the village.

Now the people realized that they had a great excess of food, for it seemed the fairy fishermen were much more successful than their human brethren, the fairy dairymaids could coax curds from milk much faster than the best farm wife, and the skill with which the fairies could climb the rocks to plunder the nests of guillemot and gannet was far beyond that of any mortal. No sooner had the people said that perhaps they should sell the excess at market than they saw there was already a cart packed ready, with a donkey lashed to it. Two men drove the cart off to market and returned with more money than any of them had seen in their lives. Their neighbours spent another day in music and storytelling, companionship and contentment.

The next day brought more of the same, but this time a great number of feathers had been plucked and stuffed into sacks, all the fleece in the village had been spun into the finest thread, and great lengths of fabric had been woven. Again the men took the work to market, and again they returned with more wealth than the village had ever known.

On and on this continued, until the village was prosperous and contented. Still it continued, and soon the villagers grew tired of being idle and began instead to be bored. There was no fleece to spin, no cloth to weave. No one could make a straw cross for St Bridget, for as soon as they thought of it, it was done. There was no fiddle to tune, no bagpipe to repair, and no need of the lovely old work songs any more, for there was no cow to milk, no butter to churn, no boat to row. An old man died one night, and his family awoke to find him washed and laid out, his coffin built and his grave dug before dawn.

"What can we do?" the villagers asked one another. "We don't mean to be ungrateful, but how can we make the fairies leave us alone?"

The more the people wondered, the more efficient the fairies became. Soon there was too much cheese to take to market, too many fish, too much cloth. The villagers were sick with food and wept and wailed.

In the end they sent for a woman who had the second sight.

"We're cursed, Ealasaid," they said. "What can we do?"

"There's only one thing to do," the old woman said. "You must defeat the fairies. Set them a task they cannot complete. Only then will they leave you alone."

All this time the boy who had called down the curse upon their heads had kept quiet. The joy he had felt at first had turned to a deep, burning shame in the pit of his stomach. Now he saw what his laziness had done, he finally understood that work is good, for through work we earn the peace of our rest. He put his mind to work now, desperate to find a way out of this dreadful predicament.

All the while the fairies worked on, never seen, never heard, achieving miraculous feats while the people lay in their restless beds, dreaming uneasy dreams.

I know! the boy thought one morning. *I've got it.*

He put on his fine new shoes, ate the hot porridge waiting in the pot on the great chain above the fire, and took himself down to the shore. All that day he sat there, fiddling with great handfuls of sand. His neighbours drifted down to fetch the fairies' catch and their feathers, the piles of salted seabirds and barrels of oil.

"*Dè tha thu ris, 'ille?*" they asked. What are you doing, lad?

"I'm trying," the boy said, "to weave a rope from this sand, but I don't have the trick of it yet."

The others shook their heads and left him to it.

That night the boy did not sleep. He lay with his eyes closed, for he had no wish to see the fairies, but he listened. He heard sounds of great industry, and then wails of frustration. Finally, as morning drew near, he heard a terrible lamenting sound, and only then did he risk a peek through the oiled cloth of the window.

In a long chain, the fairies were leaving the place, lamenting and mourning. Behind them, on the shore, were hundreds upon hundreds of lines in the sand, where they had tried and failed to weave the grains into strong pleats of rope. The boy's heart was heavy, and he wished he could call out his thanks, but he knew that his mother and father would wake to find they had no son any more, for the fairies would spirit away anyone so foolish as to cross their path. He could not do that to his parents, not after everything else he had done. And so he let the fairies go without a word of thanks.

When the village stirred the next morning, the

fires were dark and cold. The cows were lowing in the byres, heavy with milk, and the sheep cried for their winter feed. With joy in their hearts, the villagers set to and began to kindle the fires, filling their pots with a good breakfast to sustain them through the day of hard work that was before them.

Although he had passed a sleepless night the night before, the boy worked hardest of all. His hands were red and sore come nightfall, his back ached and his feet were heavy. For the first time in his young life, he said his prayers, sank into bed and knew the deep and peaceful sleep of one who has truly earned his rest.

Tam Lin

The tale of Tam Lin is told in one of the great Border Ballads, and this retelling steals pieces here and there from different versions of the song. Sometimes the fairy knight's name is Tam Lyn, or Tamlane, and sometimes he is called Tammas (Thomas). Sometimes Janet is called Margaret.

Among the rolling green hills of the Borders, where the Yarrow meets the Ettrick Water, you will find the forest of Carterhaugh. Deep within the trees lies a mossy hollow, hidden from all but those who know to seek it out. A well sings sweetly in this secret place, among the ferns and bracken. There was once magic here, and a song warned young women to stay well clear...

"O I forbid ye, maidens a',
That wear gold on your hair,
To come or go by Carterhaugh,
For young Tam Lin is there."

Tam Lin was once a mortal man, the grandson of the great Laird of Roxburgh, but many years had passed since he had vanished one afternoon while hunting in the forest. Since then he had been seen but rarely, and then only if a young woman chanced to pass through Carterhaugh. Tam Lin would appear and bar her way until she gave up a ring or a haircomb or another precious treasure. The young women whispered to one another of the ghostly knight, and soon no one went there at all.

Perhaps Janet was bolder than most, or sillier

or more headstrong, for she would not heed any warnings to stay away from Carterhaugh. The forest lay within her father's estate, after all, and why should she not walk in such a pleasant place on an autumn afternoon? And so Janet dressed in her fine green velvet gown, fastened her cloak with a crystal brooch, and plaited her golden hair. Then she kilted her skirts above her knee and set off into the forest.

It was a fine, fresh day and the way was pleasant. Janet broke a wand of hazel to make her way through the densest of the trees, and soon she was wandering deeper and deeper into the forest. The Michaelmas daisies were in bloom, starring the ground here and there. The birds sang in the leaves and now and then Janet glimpsed a deer, pausing for a startled second among the branches before it darted away.

As she neared the well in the hollow at the heart of the forest, Janet began to grow tired. It seemed warm here, and quiet, as though even the birds had stilled their song. Through the trees she saw a flash of white and then a milk-white mare went by, her head held high and her tail tossing. In her wake Janet saw a bush of wild white roses. She picked a double bloom to tuck into her hair, sat down on a tree trunk and closed her eyes.

When Janet woke from her doze, there was a new intensity to the silence in the forest. She scrambled to her feet and looked around. A tall young man stepped from behind a tree and spoke to her:

"Why pulls thou the rose, Janet,
And why breaks thou the wand?
Or why comes thou to Carterhaugh
Withoutten my command?"

Janet raised her chin.

"Carterhaugh belongs to me," she said. "This is my father's land. I will come and go here as I please. I need not ask your permission."

"My mistress's power is greater than your father's," said the young man, and Janet thought he looked a little sad.

"Who is your mistress," Janet demanded, "to consider herself so high?"

"My mistress is the Queen of the Fairies," said the young man. "She dwells in a green hill nearby."

"And who are you?" said Janet, although she had an idea that this was the ghostly knight of the women's tales.

"I'm Tam Lin," the young man told her, "and once I

was grandson to the Laird of Roxburgh. My mistress stole me away one day when I fell from my horse at the hunt. She made me a knight of her elven company and bade me guard this forest of Carterhaugh. That is why I must collect a toll from you, for you have taken her roses and stolen her hazel wand."

"*My* roses," said Janet. "*My* wand." There was no bitterness in the squabble, for Tam Lin's kind face and sad story spoke to Janet's heart in a way she had never known before.

"Give me the brooch from your cloak," said Tam Lin. "Then the toll will be paid."

"I will not," said Janet. "But I will give you my heart, for I think you need a friend."

"Do I?" said Tam Lin, and his face was sadder than any face Janet had ever seen. Then he smiled a weary smile. "I would indeed like a friend," he said, "but we have met too late, Janet. Every seven years, the fairies give one of their people as a *teind*, a rent payment to Hell. It is Halloween, the payment is due this very night, and I fear that *I* will be the *teind*."

"No!" said Janet, and she struck the ground with her hazel wand. "I won't let that happen. This place is mine, and I plan to levy my own toll – you're mine too!"

Tam Lin grinned but then he looked solemn again. "Collecting that toll will cost you dear," he said. "Are you sure you think the prize is worth it?" He looked very uncertain.

"I think so," said Janet, and the warmth of her love for him spread through her. "Tell me what to do to save you, Tam Lin."

And so Tam Lin told her. That night he would ride out in a company of knights, the eleventh and last of all. His horse would be white, while the others rode blacks and piebald greys. Janet should pull him down from his mount as he passed and hold on tight.

"Then your courage will surely be tested," he said, and he would not tell her any more.

That night Janet hid at Miles Cross, a little way from Caterhaugh. Just before midnight, she heard light hoofbeats and silver bells, and the eeriest of music that had no place in the mortal world raised goosebumps all along her arms. Soon the Queen of the Fairies and her retinue came into view. The queen rode at the head of the procession in a gown of silver, her long dark hair loose about her shoulders and a fine, silky cloak floating behind her. Then came other finely-attired women attendants and a retinue of handsome knights – two, four, six, eight, ten – and a last one in the rear, mounted on a milk-white mare. Janet bolted forward and pulled Tam Lin off the horse to the ground, rolling with him across the grass. She wrapped her arms tight around him while her heart thudded in her chest.

"Don't let go!" said Tam Lin. "No matter what happens."

By now the procession was in chaos. The music and ringing bells had stopped and the elves were all a-chatter. Then a shadow came between Janet and the moon.

"So," said the Queen of the Fairies, with a smile as cold as ice. "You think to have the bonniest knight in all my company?" She waved a silver wand and Tam Lin was turned into a wild hound in Janet's arms. He writhed and struggled, his dreadful jaws inches from Janet's face, but she held fast.

"Too easy," said the queen, and she waved her wand again. This time Tam Lin became a great lion. His roar turned Janet's blood cold, but she held to the thought that he was her true love and he would not hurt her.

"Brave, foolish girl," said the queen, and with another wave of her wand Tam Lin became a giant bear and clawed and kicked at Janet, but she would not let go.

"Is it a little chilly?" the queen said to one of her elves, and suddenly Tam Lin became a red-hot iron in Janet's arms. She smelled the hair on her arms singeing with the heat, but she closed her eyes and told herself again that her love would not hurt her, and so it was.

At last the queen turned Tam Lin into a burning coal, and Janet dropped him into a pool of water nearby. He rose up a mortal man, naked as the day he was born, and Janet wrapped him in her cloak and held him in her arms.

The Queen of the Fairies turned her icy stare on Janet.

"Shame on you, girl," she said, "to take what was not yours. An ill death may you die."

Janet's eyes watered at the woman's hatred, but she set her chin and glared back twice as hard. "He was not yours in the first place," she muttered.

The queen ignored her and turned to Tam Lin.

"Had I known what would happen this night," she said, "I would have plucked out your two grey eyes and set lumps of wood in your head in their place."

The queen turned on her heel and, with a sharp

wave of her hand, summoned the company to follow. They mounted their horses and rode off into the Borders night to pay their terrible price to the Devil. One knight seemed slow to follow the others, and Janet wondered if he would now be the *teind* in place of Tam Lin.

When at last the jingle of their harness had faded into the darkness, Janet and Tam Lin sat for a moment by the pool, suddenly shy and then overjoyed. Janet offered her hand to Tam Lin and took him home. They lived there happily ever after, and they never saw the Queen of the Fairies again, although each year they made sure the doors were locked and barred tight after dark, come Halloween.

Whuppity Stoorie

This is a story of a kind known across the world as the "Name of the Helper". If it seems familiar, you might know a famous German version called "Rumpelstiltskin". This one comes from the tradition of the Scottish Lowlands and would have been originally told in Scots. In the healing charm – written new for this book – there is one Gaelic word, "piseach". It means "improvement", usually in health.

Once upon a time, a poor young woman lived in a house in the middle of nowhere at all. This young woman wasn't precisely a wife, and she wasn't precisely a widow. She had been married, but one day her husband had disappeared. Perhaps he had taken the king's shilling and marched off in a soldier's uniform to far-flung lands. Perhaps he had gone into the navy and sailed the world. In truth, she had no idea where he was. The ground might as well have opened up below his feet and swallowed him whole for all she could explain his disappearance.

This husband had left the woman with a little son, and he was the dearest joy in her heart. He was a fine, strong boy, and the woman cared for him as well as anyone could. She would go hungry to make sure he had enough to eat. She would wear rags if it meant she could sew him a warmer shirt. She would sleep beside his bed to stop the draughts finding him. She looked after him so well that, poor as they were, no ill ever befell him.

The only wealth the woman and her son had in the world was a sow. The sow was a happy creature and had given them litter after litter of piglets to sell at market, and that money had kept just enough food in their bellies to make sure they never starved. Now the sow was old and there would be no more piglets, but she helped churn over the vegetable patch and grunted so happily in the sun that the woman and her son laughed with sheer delight. The sow was like a third member of the little family.

Then, one year, a hard winter came, as hard winters will, and the woman and her son had neither food to eat nor fuel for their fire. With a heavy heart the woman decided that she must sell the sow. The little money the beast would fetch would see them through until spring. The woman could not bear to think any further than that.

When the woman went out to the byre to fetch the pig for market, the poor beast was lying on her back with her four legs straight up in the air. It looked as though the sow was about to grunt her last.

The woman had no idea what to do to help the sow and she could not bear to see the faithful creature in pain. All her hopes of staving off her own and her boy's hunger were dashed, and in despair she sank down on a stool and began to weep. "What can I do, oh, what can I do?" she wept. "I'm so sorry, piggy! You've kept us going for so long and now we are all undone!"

Eventually the woman cried herself quiet and the sow's grunts subsided. As the woman raised her eyes to see whether the animal was dead, a strange wee creature darted past her to the far corner of the byre. The woman started in fright so that she unbalanced and fell on the floor.

At the sight of the woman sprawled on the ground, the little creature laughed. It laughed until it seemed that it would burst, and still it laughed. The woman got up and rubbed her bottom.

"I don't know what's so funny," she said, and sat down again on the stool, warily eyeing her visitor.

The creature appeared to be in the form of a woman, only very small. She wore a strange woollen gown and a cloak of sorts, made of animal skin. Around her head she wore a fine cloth of green. When she had finally finished laughing, she unwound the tail of this head cloth and used it to dry her eyes.

"I know all about you and your troubles, farm wife," she said, "and I've come to help you. You and your half-expired porcine friend."

"Pardon?" said the woman.

"Your pig," said the creature. "Dry your eyes. I can make it better and you can take it to market and sell it, and then all of your worries will be at an end and you can go back to eking out your miserable existence. If you'd like."

"Yes, please," said the woman, too grateful to notice the scornful tone in the creature's voice or the rudeness of her words. "Please help. I'll give you anything you want in return."

"Oh," said the creature, with a glint in her eye. "That's very good of you."

Then the creature got up and went over to the sow, which by now looked more dead than alive. The woman could not even be sure it was breathing. The creature poked the sow here and there, provoking a grunt or two in return. Then she took out a little bottle from a pocket in her cloak and poured some drops into the sow's mouth. She poured more on to her fingers and rubbed it on the pig's nose, its ears and the tip of its tail.

"Pitter, potter, healing water," she said. "Pitter, potter, *PISEACH*!" She put the bottle back in her pocket and clapped her hands. "On your feet, pig!" she said. "Come on!"

The woman couldn't believe her eyes. Her faithful friend was standing on its four feet and running round the byre as though it were a young piglet again instead of a worn-out old sow. Her heart filled with joy and tears spilled from her eyes.

"You have saved me," she said to the mysterious creature. "What can I give you to show you my thanks?"

"That's easy," said the creature. "I want your little boy."

"My son?" the woman said, turned stupid by surprise. "But you can't mean it. You can't take my son!"

The creature cocked its head to one side. "*Anything*, that's what you said," it said. "Or should I undo the magic and let the sow die?"

Now the woman really was in a bind, for what good would it do her to keep her son if all that she could do for the child was to let him starve? She fell again to crying and weeping while the creature watched with interest.

"I'm not hard-hearted," the creature said. "I'll tell you what. I'll give you three days with your boy. In those three days, if you can guess my name, I'll let you keep the child and you'll never see me again. But when I return, if you have not guessed, I will take the boy."

With a laugh, the creature ran out of the door of

the byre and down the brae from the house. The woman settled the sow into a bed of straw and took herself off to bed. She cuddled into her son's warm blankets and, worn out, she fell asleep.

The woman woke early. All that day she puzzled out how she might find out the name of the creature that had helped her. She made a list in her head of all of the names she had ever heard. She took down her Bible from the shelf and began to read the names in it, but then she stopped, for she thought that the creature had different beliefs and her name would not be found there.

By the end of the first day, the woman was no closer to guessing the name. She passed a sleepless night and worried all the next day. She barely slept at all the second night, for she knew that the next day would bring the creature back, and it would be time to guess, or lose her son for ever. As she stirred a pot of thin porridge for their breakfast, her head bobbed with tiredness. "Let's eat," she said to her son. "And once we've eaten, we'll take ourselves out for a walk." To herself, she thought sadly, *We might as well enjoy our last day together.*

They pulled on their hats and their scarves and their warmest clothes and they trudged out into the snow. They lived by a great forest, and when they reached the forest the woman picked up the boy and walked with him balanced on her shoulders. They walked deeper and deeper into the trees, and then the woman heard a coarse crowing noise coming from a little away.

A few steps further on, the woman saw the strange creature sitting on a tree stump, with a basket of fleece by her feet and a spindle by her side. She was carding the fleece and singing, rocking to and fro. It took the woman a moment to understand the words of her song:

"She knows not what my name may be,
she'll never guess at Whuppity Stoorie."

Whuppity Stoorie, the woman thought to herself, delighted at her luck. *Her name is Whuppity Stoorie!* She caught up her son and crept out of the forest and back home.

That evening, the creature knocked on the door and the woman bade her enter. The woman's heart sang with joy, but she made sure her face was grave.

"Well, mistress," the creature said. "Give me the bairn."

"Not so fast," the woman answered. "You said I could try to guess at your name."

The creature smiled a nasty smile.

"So I did," she said. "Go on. I'm feeling generous, so I'll give you three guesses."

The woman knew there was no generosity in the creature's heart, and so she decided to have some fun with her.

"My first guess is . . . Tattie Bogle," she said. That was a word for a scarecrow, and she guessed the creature would be offended, for she seemed to like fine clothes.

"Cheek!" the creature said. "NO!"

"My second guess is . . . Glaikit Sumph," the woman said. Now she was really having fun, as this was an insult for a stupid, lazy person.

"NO!" the creature roared. "You don't have the first idea, do you?" And she grinned a horrible grin.

"No," said the woman, "but I would still like my third guess. I'll guess . . . let's see . . . hang on . . . WHUPPITY STOORIE!"

As soon as the woman spoke the name, the creature began to let out the most dreadful howling and caterwauling. She began to spin around and around, faster and faster, until finally she lifted off the ground and flew out of the byre and away.

The woman never did see Whuppity Stoorie again. She and her son lived peacefully and happily, with plenty to eat, since their old sow was now like a young beast again and had many more litters over the years. They kept some of her piglets and bred from them, and in this way they made enough money that they never had to worry about hunger or hard winters ever again.

Monsters, Magical Creatures and Shapeshifters

A Scottish joke

How do you communicate with Nessie?

Answer
Drop her a line...

Scotland is a country of deep, dark waters, high, snowy mountains and islands shrouded in mist. The wind howls eerily round the steep peaks, shadows fall oddly where the light shines on cloud, and winter nights are long and dark. Perhaps this is why our stories are packed with magical creatures and shapeshifters. Some of these beings are good, but most are not. They are found on land, in the water and in the air, and they range from dragons to giant worms, to Scotland's most famous beastie of all, the Loch Ness Monster.

The Seal-wife

Stories of shapeshifters are common all across the world. Stories of women who shapeshift to human form from an original guise as a seal or mermaid are especially common in Scotland, Ireland and Scandinavia. Perhaps the stories travelled to and fro with the Vikings on their ships...

There are more than one hundred islands and skerries in the great chain that forms the Outer Hebrides, far off the west coast of Scotland in the Atlantic Ocean's roar. Among the largest of the islands are North and South Uist, lands of white sands and crystal-clear water, low, fertile machair and barley, marram grass and heather.

Once upon a time there lived a young man in North Uist who was called Pàdraig. He made his living as all his neighbours did, from the land and the sea, as a fisherman and as a crofter. Once every year, Pàdraig would leave behind his own small boat and his own green croft and help the other men launch a great boat from the west of the island, and row it out to the flat, green islet of Heisgeir, to hunt the seals.

Pàdraig did not enjoy the seal hunt, but life was hard in the islands back then. People needed meat to salt down for the weeks or months of gnawing hunger when no crops grew and no boats came. They needed warm furs to keep out the cold, and oil for the crusie lamps that kept the darkness at bay while they mended their nets and attended to the other winter work.

This one particular year, there were dozens of

seals sheltering on Heisgeir, and soon Pàdraig and the other Uistmen had taken all they needed and more. When they had loaded the boat, there were still so many carcasses left on the shore that they decided one man should stay to stand guard while the others rowed home with their haul. They would return the next day to fetch him with the second load of seals.

No one wanted to be the one to stay. There were so many stories of water bulls and sea monsters, kelpies that took the shape of horses on land and men in the sea, and strange blue spirits that lived in the water, tempting sailors to their doom. Who would wish to risk spending a night alone with the carcasses of some seals on an island so far from help and home?

In the end they drew lots. Pàdraig's straw was the shortest, and so it fell to him to stand on the beach and watch as the ship drew away through the waves. When it had slipped over the horizon and even the men's singing was lost to him on the wind, he found an overhang in the dunes above the bay and crawled inside. They had left him a blanket stiff with oil to keep out any rain that should come. He pulled it tight around him, closed his eyes and slept.

The moon was high when a sound from the shore woke Pàdraig from his slumber. The sound was long and low, eerie and inhuman, and Pàdraig felt his heart pound in his chest. He shrugged free from the blanket and crawled forward out of the dune. A cloud passed over the moon, then pale light shone once more on the foreshore and Pàdraig saw a sight that raised the fine hairs on his arm like the needles of a fir tree.

Dozens of women had appeared on the beach, long-haired and ghostly, their arms raised above their heads and a keening coming from their mouths. As Pàdraig watched, horrified and spellbound, two seals swam on to the shore, cast aside their skins and took on human form. They joined the women on the sand, mourning and lamenting as they walked among their dead kindred.

Pàdraig crept back to his hiding place in the dune and breathed deeply for a time until he could still his heart. A few moments later he was calm again, and he peeked out from the overhanging grass. That was when he spotted a sealskin, flung over a rock by the base of the dune. Later, when he looked back, he could not say precisely why he took it. It was a beautiful thing, and perhaps he wanted it for its loveliness. Perhaps he also understood it would buy him a while with the woman who owned it. At the time he did not pause to think. He simply checked the coast was clear, crawled over and snatched it. Then he bundled it in his blanket, waited and watched.

When at last the first rays of dawn kissed the horizon, the seal women turned, picked up their skins and began to make their way back to the sea. Eventually only one woman remained. She paced to and fro in panic, searching among the dead seals for her skin. When she realized it was nowhere to be found, she sank to her knees on the bloody shore and began to cry.

Pàdraig came out of his hiding place and approached the seal-maiden, crouching down and speaking gently so as not to alarm her. At first she was afraid and looked as though she might run, but Pàdraig shrank back and then gently offered his hand. After a pause she took it. He led her back to the hiding place in the dune, gave her food to eat and water to drink, and wrapped her in his blanket. By now the sealskin was stashed in a sack of his belongings, ready to load on the boat when it returned.

The other men had eyes as wide as dinner plates when they returned in the boat and found Pàdraig with the seal-maiden. They stared as he helped her aboard the boat, but they had little choice but to row her home. Pàdraig took her to his own house, where she touched every chair and lamp and pot and plate one by one, but she said never a word.

Gradually the seal-maiden learned how to light the lamps and smoor the fire, milk the cow and churn the butter, bake the bannocks and spin fleece into wool. Still she never spoke.

Months passed, and Pàdraig and the seal-maiden were married. The following year, they had a son. He was a sturdy little chap with red hair and strong lungs. They called him Codrum. Sometimes, when she thought she was alone, the seal-maiden sang to the baby with a low, wordless song, but if she caught Pàdraig watching, she closed her mouth again tight.

Pàdraig now had a pressing problem. When he had first brought the seal-maiden home, he had hidden the sealskin by the wall in the back of the stackyard, where he built the first stack at harvest. The skin was then twice concealed, for it was hidden under the stack and the stack itself was soon hidden from sight behind the others. In this way, the sealskin was safe until the end of spring, when Pàdraig would rake out the last wisps of straw from the yard. Then he would hide the skin among the fishing nets under the rafters of the byre, until such time as he could bring the harvest in again and build the stacks of fodder in the stackyard once more. And during those weeks Pàdraig slept badly, worried all the while that the skin would be found.

In this way Pàdraig and the seal-maiden passed a number of years. Codrum grew into a fine young lad. He liked nothing better than to be with his father, mending the nets or feeding the beasts, mucking out the donkey or grooming the pony. He helped his mother too, milking the cow and helping to churn golden butter and press firm white rounds of cheese. He longed to be allowed to climb up on the roof of the house to mend the thatch and weight it with anchor-stones, but Pàdraig said he was still too young, and not yet tall enough to reach.

One day Pàdraig had to go to the island to the south to fetch home a new bull. He would be gone a day and a night, waiting for low tide when it would be safe to cross the ford to the south, and then waiting until it was safe to swim the bull home again the other way. On the first afternoon, Codrum stayed close to his mother, helping with chores in the house and feeding the hens in the yard. That night, the wind blew up without warning and he lay in his box-bed listening to a storm roar and cry around the house. In the morning, the rain was still driving down but Codrum decided that a few drops of water would not put off the man of the house, and he marched off around the croft to check that all was well. The storm had left its mark – there was a great hole in the roof of the byre, where the wind had torn the thatch away.

Codrum ran into the byre and climbed up into the rafters to view the damage from inside. He pulled aside the fishing nets and weights that his father kept there, and underneath it all he had found something soft – a whole sealskin. He was enchanted – it was heavy and sleek, dense and somehow alive. With a cry of delight, he leaped down and took the treasure to his mother.

Codrum's mother's face turned almost as grey as the sealskin when she saw what it was that her son held in his arms. She took it without a word, turned and walked back into the house. Codrum felt uneasy. He ran back to the byre and found his old dog Bran. He cuddled into the dog's fur and told him everything would be all right.

When Pàdraig returned that afternoon with the bull, he found Codrum asleep in the byre. There was no sign of his wife. She was gone. Pàdraig never saw the seal-wife again, but sometimes when Codrum went to the shore he thought that a seal swam in the shadow of his footsteps, far out to sea.

Did you know that the seals can sing? If you are ever on a boat in waters where seals gather, lean over the side and sing to them. They will come to listen, and if you are lucky you will hear them answer you with a song of their own.

It is still said today that the clan MacCodrum are descended from the seal-wife's son. They have a particular talent for music and song, and people say that this is an echo in their blood of the seal-maiden's gift to her son, for the seals love music so very dearly.

The Waterhorse and the Girl

All over Scotland tales are told of water spirits or demons that can take the shape of horses to walk on land. Unwary humans persuaded to climb on these creatures' backs are carried off under the water, never to be seen again. In this way, the stories may have been used to warn young people that no good comes from straying too close to the banks of a river or loch, or from wandering off with a stranger.

This version of the story is from Barra, the southernmost island in the Outer Hebrides. The retelling mixes Gaelic tradition, in which the creatures are simply called eich uisge, *or "waterhorses", and Lowland tradition, in which they are known as "kelpies". In 2013 the largest horse sculptures in the world were unveiled near the great Forth and Clyde Canal by the town of Falkirk. These huge horse heads were named the Kelpies.*

Once upon a time, hundreds of years ago, a waterhorse lived in the deep, peaty waters of the isle of Barra. The people of Barra, the *Barraich*, told tales of the dreadful creature around the fire at night, and no one dared go near the water after dark.

This waterhorse was no horse truly seen, but a shape-shifting water spirit. When on land he could take the form of a great black horse, finely shod, and saddled and bridled in the finest leather. He had a gloss to his coat and a toss to his head worthy of the finest stallion, but he could run faster and leap higher than any horse that had ever lived, for he was constrained by no mortal weakness. He could also take on the shape of a man, with hair as dark as his horse's mane and eyes as wild as the sea.

The people thought the waterhorse evil, although none could truly know what lay in his heart. A lion may kill a man or a woman, but this is not an evil act. And so it may have been with the kelpie – he simply did what was in his nature.

One fine summer's day, a young woman ventured out to seek a cow that had gone astray. She kilted up her skirts and left the fine grazing land where the others were lazing, picking her away across rock and moor, round the fringes of lochans and inlets, and past long-deserted ruins where unknown families had once eked out a living generations before. At last she spied the cow a little way ahead, cropping contentedly on a patch of bog-cotton.

The girl was so intent on the cow that at first she did not notice a fine black horse had risen from the loch to the west of her and moved soundlessly across the moor to stand still as a stone by her side. When at last she saw the horse, still wet from the water, she shuddered, for she knew at once that this was no mortal creature. All the old charms ran through her head. What did people say to do with a kelpie? She thought it might help to call on the Holy Trinity of the church, or make the sign of the cross, or to take the kelpie's bridle and bind it in that way.

The kelpie stared at the girl, and the girl stared back, and she felt all thoughts of prayer melt from her mind. For was it not an enchanting creature, as dark and beautiful as the night itself, the water droplets shining like stars in its coat of silk? What harm could it mean her? If she just reached out and put her foot into the stirrup—

The girl shook her head, remembering the tales of

the kelpie's magic and how it used its beauty to lull its victims into a false sense of safety. *Two can play at that game*, she thought.

"*'S e each-uisge a th' annaibh*," she said aloud to the creature. *You're a waterhorse.*

The waterhorse dipped his head in acknowledgement, and the girl heard his answer in her head, for it was not spoken aloud.

"I am," the waterhorse said. "And you are best and bravest girl in all of Barra. I want to make you my wife."

The arrogance of the statement almost made the girl laugh. She was still afraid, but now a spark of defiance flamed in her heart. She was determined to keep her wits about her and teach this proud, foolish creature a lesson.

"That's very flattering," she said. "But if I am to live with you under the water, I imagine it will be very cold. I am making a shawl – see, I have the knitting with me and it is almost done. May I finish it, so that I may wear it in my new home?"

She showed the waterhorse the fine cobweb knitting and he inclined his head.

With a wary eye on the waterhorse, the girl sat on a rock and began to knit. The rhythmic clicking of the needles calmed her, and a plan began to weave itself in her mind.

"Can you take human form?" she asked conversationally.

"I can," said the waterhorse, and in the space of a heartbeat he stood before her in the form of a dark-haired man.

The girl knitted on.

"Will you not sit by me?" she said. "After all, we are to be married."

After a second's hesitation, the man sat beside her in a warm patch of sun. He did not look entirely comfortable in his human guise. The girl was torn between laughter and horror. She had no wish to fall under this creature's spell and leave behind everything she knew, but as a human she felt he was less a danger, somehow.

On the girl knitted, and after a while she began to sing. She sang every spinning song she knew, and then every lullaby she knew. Donald Gorm's lullaby, the Fairy Lullaby, Bà bà My Little Child... On and on she sang:

"Bidh clann an rìgh
seinnear a' phìob

òlar am fìon
air do bhainis."

The king's children will be there
the pipes will sound
wine will flow
for your wedding.

The sun grew warmer and warmer, the needles clicked out the beat of a heart and the songs grew sleepier and sleepier. Exactly as the girl had planned, the kelpie's head began to nod and then he was asleep.

Moving as gently and as silently as she could, the girl lifted the shirt from the kelpie's neck and saw that he wore a silver chain there. She had half a memory that a kelpie could be controlled by whoever held his bridle and she hoped against hope that this was true. She unfastened the chain, clasped it around her own neck, picked up her knitting and carried on.

As the afternoon grew colder, the kelpie awoke. He said not a word, but stared mutely at the girl and his chain around her neck with eyes that held all the sadness of the ages. It seemed he could no longer speak.

"I have your bridle," the girl said, "but you need not be afraid of me. Come, I'll take you home."

The girl began to drive the cow home before her, and the kelpie followed at her heels. He was as meek as a kitten, and spoke not one word all the long way back.

At home, the girl fetched a halter from the byre and placed it around the kelpie's neck. Immediately he became a horse again, as fine to look at as he was before, but obedient and biddable. For a year and a day he lived with them and he was the best horse they had ever owned. He pulled their plough with ease through the rocky soil. He carried peats home on his back from the moor, and seaweed from the shore. They were able to help their neighbours too, and the village prospered. At night the girl sat in the byre where he was stabled and looked in his eyes, and she saw the kelpie looking back. It was an odd feeling – she fancied that his eyes had grown warmer and softer, lost a little of the wildness of the sea. She felt that he knew her, and liked her, and she found that she wished he could become a man again so that they could sit together by the fire of a winter's night and talk until morning.

When the year and one day had passed and

summer had come again, the girl knew she could no longer keep the kelpie in her power. With a heavy heart, she took hold of his halter and led him around the bay to the house where old Annag lived. Annag had the gift of *an dà shealladh* – the second sight – and if anyone would know what should be done, the girl knew that it would be Annag.

It was a fine day, and warm, the air heavy with the scent of heather and the industrious buzzing of the bees. As they neared Annag's house, they saw that the old woman was sitting by her door with her spinning wheel and a basket of fleece. She stood up as they approached and peered closely at the kelpie.

"Take that halter off the beast, *a nighean*," she said to the girl.

After a second's pause, the girl did as she was told.

"Do you have the chain?" the old woman asked.

The girl unclasped the chain from her neck where she had worn it ever since she had first bound the kelpie. She passed it to Annag, still warm from her skin.

In the space of a heartbeat, the kelpie became a man again. He shook his head and rolled his shoulders and stared at the women warily.

"I have your bridle, kelpie," Annag said, and she

held the chain at arms' length. "Would you like it back?"

At that the girl started, for it had become second nature to her to ensure that the kelpie was bound. Annag put out a hand to signal her to be still.

The kelpie spoke to Annag, but he looked at the girl. "You may keep hold of it for now," he said. "If you feel safer that way."

"Very well," said Annag, and she dropped the chain into her other hand. "Do you want it back at all?"

"I do," said the kelpie, "and I do not. The last year has been like no other year I have ever known. I am a solitary creature by nature, but I have spent a year in the company of others. I have no employment where I live, but here I have been useful. My home is cold and dark and watery, but here I have seen the seasons change and have lived in the light."

"Have you been treated well?" Annag asked. "For you are a powerful creature, I think, to have been bound so long."

"I have been treated better than I deserved," said the kelpie. "I toiled for my people, and they fed and sheltered me in return. I have been shown respect and kindness, and I have come to see that *before* I was not used to treating others in the same way. I see now that I have been arrogant and selfish. I thought I could take anything I needed or wanted without paying any price or politeness for it. I thought I could take this girl to be my wife without asking her preference in the matter. I see now that I was wrong."

"You have learned much, I think," said Annag. "What is your wish now? Do you wish to go home to your watery place? Do you wish to stay on land? And what will you be? A man? A horse? A water spirit?"

"I wish to stay on land," said the kelpie shyly. Then he seemed to grow bolder. "And I wish to be a man, because I wish to earn this girl's love. I very much hope that she will marry me one day, if I can prove myself worthy of her trust."

"What do you say to that?" Annag asked the girl.

At first the girl had no idea what to say. The kelpie had thought to force her to become his wife, and that was wrong. She had bound him and kept him, and perhaps she had not seen that she had a choice at the time, but now she could see that that had also been wrong. There was much that was wrong between them, but there was also a gentle tenderness, and her heart warmed when she looked in his eyes.

Those eyes were no longer the cold, slate-grey of the sea in a storm. They were blue and bright, and they stared uncertainly into her own.

"I would like that very much," she said, and she almost laughed as the kelpie smiled a smile that suggested he had not had much practice at smiling before. Then he was laughing too, and Annag shook her head and reached out her hand to the kelpie.

"Here," she said. "Your bridle."

The kelpie took the silver chain and gave it to the girl. "Will you mind this for me?" he asked. "If I give it to you as a gift, it will not bind my lips as it did before. I will trust you to keep it safe, in thanks for the great trust you have placed in me."

"I will," the girl said, "and I know that I will never need to touch it again, for as long as we both shall live."

Then they ran off into the heat of the day, towards the rest of their long and happy lives.

Mester Stoor Worm

From the 800s until the 1400s, the Northern Isles of Orkney and Shetland were part of Norway. Even after the islands formally became part of Scotland, they retained strong links with Scandinavia, and many of their stories – including this one – have strong roots in Scandinavian lore and belief.

Once upon a time, in the dark depths of the cold North Sea, there lived a dreadful creature called the Mester Stoor Worm. How he came to live there no one knew, but everyone who had ever heard his name understood that he was a curse upon humankind. His breath was poison to anyone who got near enough to smell it. He had a huge tail that could drown entire fleets of ships as easily as you might knock a glass off a table – *SPLASH!* His great mouth contained a terrible tongue that might lick a city off the face of a hillside – *SLURP!* – or bore a hole in a castle wall and suck everyone inside into his gaping maw – *CRUNCH!*

Most of the time the Stoor Worm lived many fathoms deep, but when he grew hungry he would swim into shallower waters and come to rest near a great city. The people of the unfortunate country to which that city belonged were then charged with feeding the Stoor Worm. For unless his dreadful hunger was satisfied, they knew that their city and all its people would be wiped off the face of the earth.

Every seven nights, the Stoor Worm would wake, open his terrible mouth and yawn nine times. Then he would demand a meal of seven maidens. Only the loveliest would do, for despite his ugly appearance, he had dainty tastes.

A long time ago, the Stoor Worm settled near the shore of an ancient country in the far north. Every Saturday at sunset seven girls would be given to the beast, and every Saturday he would eat the poor girls up and spit out their shoes.

Perhaps the Stoor Worm stayed too long in this one place, or perhaps they were a bold people, for soon this country grew tired of giving up their daughters. They went to the elders of the land and said that it would no longer do. The elders went to the Stoor Worm to plead with him to leave them alone. The Stoor Worm agreed – if first he could have the daughter of the king for his dinner.

When the elders put this proposal to the king, he refused. His daughter was his only living child and he loved her dearly. He pleaded and begged with the elders, but they were resolute. In the end they agreed to give him ten weeks to spend with his child before she would be given to the Stoor Worm.

No sooner had the ten weeks begun than the king sent to every corner of his kingdom, offering a handsome reward to any hero who would slay the Stoor Worm. He promised money, he promised land

and he promised the hand of his beloved daughter. He also promised that the hero would be given his most prized possession, the sword *Sikkersnapper.* The king had inherited this sword from the great Odin himself, the one-eyed god of wisdom and war.

Warriors flooded from every corner of the kingdom to take up the challenge. Upon seeing the Stoor Worm, all but twelve changed their minds immediately and returned home to take up their hoes and their ploughs and never again to think of deeds of valour. Of the twelve remaining, the first died in the Stoor Worm's maw. The second drowned under his tail. The third perished on his breath. The remaining nine turned tail and fled.

Frantically, the king sent his heralds on his fastest horses to seek new heroes. None would come.

On the ninth day, a farm boy arrived at the king's house. His name was Assipattle and he was the seventh son of a seventh son. He lived with his six brothers, his mother and his uncles on a farm by a stream. The family worked hard to feed the many mouths in the house, but Assipattle rarely joined in. Instead he preferred to lie in the ashes by the fire and dream. He dreamed of great feats of daring, gods and monsters, magic and mayhem, and the stories seemed so real in his head that he wanted to share them with anyone who would listen. But when he tried to tell his brothers they just laughed and cuffed him around the ear. They told him he was a fool, and a lazy one at that.

When Assipattle heard of the king's plight, he decided that he would help. He slipped away from home in the dead of night, taking only his little boat and a bucket containing a glowing peat from the fire. The king told him where to find the monster, and Assipattle got into his boat with his bucket and rowed out towards it.

As Assipattle neared the monster, he saw how the part of its dreadful body that curved out of the water filled the whole bay, but was still dwarfed by the parts that shimmered below the waves. Its head was as big as the volcano behind his family's house, and its eyes were as cold as the glaciers where he had played as a boy.

The sun began to rise and the creature yawned in anticipation of its forthcoming meal. With every yawn the monster swallowed a vast wall of water, and finally Assipattle was close enough to be swallowed up, boat and all.

Assipattle paddled his little boat through the

cave of the creature's mouth, down the passage of its throat and into the dark, twisting tunnels of its innards. For mile after mile he paddled on, swept by the water, while the dreadful juices of the beast's insides gurgled. At last the boat beached on solid ground . . . or solid *something*. Assipattle climbed from the boat, grabbed his bucket, and ran faster than he had ever run before. He ran past unspeakable smells and rotting messes, gases and gushes and twists and turns. At last he found the creature's liver. He pulled out a knife and cut into the giant organ, and then he stuffed the peat inside.

Once the peat was inside, Assipattle blew and blew with all his might, terrified that the peat would not kindle back to life. Peat burns long and slow, and finally his patience was rewarded. The peat spluttered into life, the liver made a dreadful crackle, and soon it was blazing like a star.

Assipattle ran at full tilt back to his little boat and clambered aboard. No sooner was he seated inside than the Stoor Worm gave a great heave as the pain in its liver made it sick to its stomach. Assipattle was carried in his sturdy little boat on a great tide of acid and water back towards the beast's mouth, where he was spewed out and hurtled back into the sea. He managed to steer his faithful boat to shore, where he promptly jumped into the water to wash the worst of the foulness from his clothes.

By the time Assipattle was clean again, a great crowd had gathered to watch the struggles of the Stoor Worm. Smoke billowed from its nostrils and it heaved here and there in a vain attempt to quell the fire within. Its forked tongue shot out and caught on a star in the heavens, which crashed to earth and made a deep rift where it fell. The waters ran into this rift and formed the Baltic Sea.

As the fire grew hotter, the Stoor Worm writhed and twisted in agony, thrashing its head off the ground in its dreadful death throes. Teeth fell from its mouth and landed in the sea, where they formed the Orkney Islands. More showered out to the north to form the islands of Shetland. A final heave brought forth the far-off Faroes.

With a last great howl, the Stoor Worm cast itself far into the waves. It died where it fell, and the spiny parts that remained above the face of the ocean, burned black and smoking, became the land of Iceland.

It took some hours for the sky to clear from smoke and the people to clear the debris of the beast's death. Once the sky shone bright again, the king took Assipattle in his arms and called him a hero. He presented him with *Sikkersnapper* and offered him the hand of the princess. The princess was a lover of stories and was well pleased with the arrangement.

Assipattle and the princess were married with great feasting and celebration. Boats were burned and songs were sung, and every man, woman and child in the kingdom vowed that they would never forget how lucky they were, for the Mester Stoor Worm was finally dead and gone, and they could live together in peace once more.

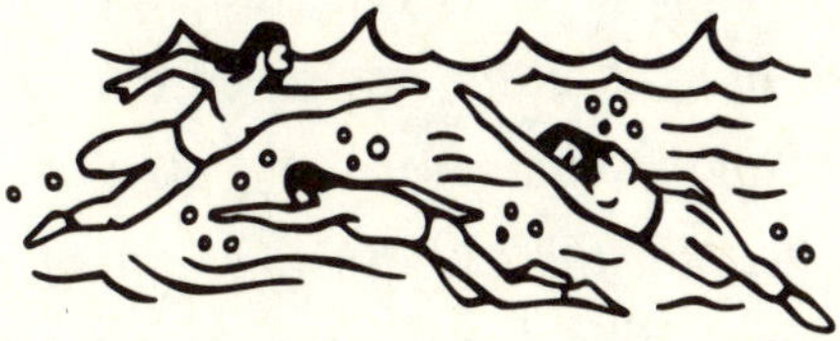

The Blue Men of the Minch

Most shape-shifters and supernatural beings in Scottish folklore appear in stories in multiple locations across the country. Na Fir Ghorma, *or the Blue Men of the Minch, are an exception. They only appear in stories from the Western Isles, connected to one particular body of water. No one knows the origins of the story, but there are some interesting theories. The Vikings brought African slaves to Scottish shores, and in Gaelic the word "gorm" is used to describe black skin, although it can mean a spectrum of colours from greeny-blue to glossy blue-black. Taken together, some people say that these two facts suggest that local people named the place the Vikings moored their boats* Sruth nam Fear Gorma – *"the Tide-stream of the Blue Men" – and the name remained once the Vikings and their African prisoners were long forgotten. The story was then created, the theory goes, to explain the meaning of the old name for this dangerous stretch of water.*

The Minch, *An Cuan Sgìth*, separates the Scottish mainland from the north-westerly islands of Lewis and Harris. It is a wild stretch of water where even the most seasoned mariner has cause to be wary, for storms and squalls blow up to toss boats here and there, and a careless skipper might easily steer his ship to splinters upon the skerries. The water is home to porpoises, dolphins and minke whales, and the air is alive with fulmars and gannets, puffins, kittiwakes and razorbills. The great Arctic skua is the scourge of the skies, but every now and then even these great brown beasts are dwarfed completely by a soaring sea eagle, with a wingspan so great it seems to block out the very sun.

Many lives have been lost in the Minch and stories of hauntings and disappearances are carried on the waves. These are human stories, though, and the Minch is the domain of otherworldly beings too. A legend says that many generations ago, a host of angels fell from heaven to land upon the earth. Some of these angels went to dwell under the ground in magical hills with doors that open – sometimes – into the human world. They are known as the little people, or *na sìthichean* – the fairies.

A second group of angels were unwilling to give up their gift of flight, and so they took up residence in the skies. They are the *Fir Chlis*, the Merry Dancers, and they may be seen over Scotland and north to Scandinavia on cold winter nights as they flicker here and there, green and pink and blue and gold. In Latin they are called the Aurora Borealis, and in English the Northern Lights.

Still more of the fairies fell into the sea, and they became the Blue Men of the Minch. Like the rest of their fallen kindred, they have little love for mortal creatures, and no sailor wishes to meet them as he crosses the treacherous waters of the strait.

It is said that the Blue Men live in caves below the deep waters by the Shiants and the waters above their home flow fast and fierce regardless of the weather, dragging ships down to their doom. They are coloured grey-blue like the sea, with long faces and grey beards. When the water is calm they float gently below the surface and pass the time in conversation and sport, being partial especially to a game of shinty. They are fine and witty poets and have been known to challenge a skipper to finish a rhyme ... or lose his ship to the deep. Their leader is called Shony, and he is their finest rhymer and most fearsome fighter. Like the fairies, the Blue Men respect rules, and if a sailor can match Shony's rhyming, line by line, they will keep their side of the bargain and let him go.

Once upon a time, a group of sailors was crossing the Minch when they spied a strange creature following in their wake. At first they mistook it for a porpoise, for it leaped and twisted in the waves, poking its head clear of the spray to flip and twist around. They saw that it looked like a human, only blue, but it swam and skipped along in the wild wake of the ship at a speed no mortal creature could possibly achieve.

The men fetched a net and, with some difficulty, they cast it out behind the boat and caught the skipping creature in its folds. They hauled the net back on board with the creature inside and laid it on the deck. Now that it was close enough to inspect they saw that they were right and the creature was indeed shaped like a human, but it was as blue as the waves themselves. It lay trapped in the net and glared at them with its green-grey eyes.

"We should throw it back to where it came from," one man said. "No good can come of having such a creature on board."

"No," said the skipper. "We don't know what it means to do. It may drag us down with it into the deeps."

"We should take it home and ask the minister what to do," a third man said.

They all nodded at that, despite their misgivings, for their minister was the wisest man they knew.

"We can't leave it there in a net like a herring till we get home," said a third man. "That's no way to treat a magical creature."

"No, it is not," said the skipper. "But still we must bind its hands and its feet with rope." He peered at the creature. "If you don't struggle," he said, "we won't hurt you."

One man fetched a rope while the others took the creature from the net and held it still on the deck. They bound its hands and its feet, and it lay there like a landed fish, although it could breathe perfectly well out of the water. It glared but it did not speak. It jerked its head in anger and the men heard an ominous roll of thunder overhead. The sky grew dark and there was a smell in the air that spoke of danger to come.

The men felt fear in the pit of their bellies, and they hurried to turn the boat and head back to harbour.

The wind was rising as they had never heard it rise before, and they struggled to reef the sails ready to weather the storm.

Some little way on, while the full circle of the sea still surrounded them and the spray blinded them and there was no land to see in any direction, one of the men called out in alarm. The others abandoned their tasks and lurched across the slippery deck to join him in the stern. He pointed into the waves and they peered through the darkening afternoon.

Two blue shapes were bouncing through the angry sea, rising proud from the spray, screeching and laughing in wild abandon.

"Heaven help us," the skipper cried. "There are two more of them!"

Over the roar of the waves, the sailors heard the Blue Men call to one another.

"Donald will be one man!" one of them cried to the other.

"Duncan will be the other!" his companion called back.

"What do they mean?" the skipper cried. "What do they plan to do?"

Before the sailors had a chance to answer, the Blue Man on the deck leaped on his feet as though the ropes that had bound him were woven from nothing stronger than sand. He shouted in a deep roar, "Donald's voice I hear, and Duncan too is near. But no need of help has mighty Iain Mòr!"

Then the Blue Man called Iain Mòr ran past the sailors. He cleared the side of the boat and landed with a great splash by his fellows in the sea. He shook an angry fist at the sailors.

"Count yourselves lucky, lads!" he roared, "for you would never have made it home with me!" Then he and his friends leaped out of the water like porpoises, turned in mid-air and headed back the way they had come. As soon as they were out of sight, the wind died down and the sea grew calm again.

"I never wanted to come to sea," the eldest crewman said. "A field of barley and a cow, that's all I ever wanted."

"Me neither," said the youngest man. "But my brother has my father's croft and I had little choice."

"The sea is my greatest love," said the skipper, "but I have always known that she is a hard mistress, and today I feared she would call in the debt I owe to her." Then he shook his head. "Heave to, lads," he said, "for I think we'll all welcome dry land under our feet tonight."

They sailed home in safety, and no man of that crew ever cast his nets into the deep again without a quick prayer under his breath, and a second glance at the haul he pulled back in again.

Scotland and Ireland and Scandinavia

A Gaelic saying:

People will meet, but mountains will not.

In common with many countries, Scotland has been shaped by its neighbours through the centuries. To the south our closest neighbour, England, has been a friend and a foe. Many traditional stories – such as the one about Tam Lin – are found on both sides of the border. England does not, however, appear often as a setting in our traditional stories. Perhaps this is because stories are set "once upon a time", before the country we know as England today got its name. Instead the countries that appear are Ireland and "Lochlann", the countries of modern-day Scandinavia.

Irish people first crossed into Scotland to settle around 200 AD, and over the next centuries Gaelic language and culture spread across the country. Many of our stories call on this shared cultural heritage.

Around six hundred years after Irish settlers arrived, Norse raiders first began to attack coastal communities, and soon Norse settlers sailed across the sea to establish communities in the north and west. Some of our stories are shared with these neighbours, and others remember times of rivalry and conflict.

Fionn MacCumhaill and the Giant Baby

The great hero Fionn MacCumhaill appears in the Fenian Cycle, an important set of stories preserved in manuscripts written in Scotland and Ireland in the Middle Ages. Some of these stories, and other stories featuring Fionn, also appear in oral tradition in both countries into the present day. This is a very light-hearted story about Fionn and his clever wife that has become popular in Scotland, Ireland and the Isle of Man. Although it features characters from Gaelic legend, it is more often told in English.

Once upon a time there lived a great warrior called Fionn MacCumhaill. Fionn was not like other men; he was enormously tall and brave and strong, and his earthly strength was matched by magical powers. When he was a young boy, he had burned his thumb on a salmon he was cooking for his foster father on an open fire. The fish was a magical creature, the Salmon of Knowledge, and when Fionn stuck his burned thumb in his mouth, its magic transferred to him. From that day on, he only had to put his thumb in his mouth and bite down to know all there was to know in the world. He knew what was about to happen before it did, or where any lost thing might be found, or what dark plans a man held in his heart even when that man was thousands of leagues away.

Fionn was the head of a great band of other heroes called the Fianna. The Fianna roamed across Scotland and Ireland, crossing the sea by means of a giant path of stones called the Giant's Causeway that still joins the north coast of Ireland to the island of Staffa in Scotland today. They fought any man they met, and hunted and sang as they roasted the day's catch on a great fire in their camp. Their legends travelled far and wide in the stories and songs of their great bard Oisean. There were many men who dreamed of besting the great Fionn MacCumhaill, his war-band and his great hound Bran, but none succeeded.

One summer's day, when the sun split the stones with heat, Fionn was in Ireland with his wife. They had just sat down to dinner in a house they had there, when Fionn felt a great wave of unease pass across him. He bit down on his thumb, and in an instant he could feel the ground shake under his feet and the waves lap at his knees.

"There is a great giant on his way from Scotland," Fionn told his wife. "As we speak he is crossing the causeway. He has but one thought in his mind – to find Fionn MacCumhaill and rip him limb from limb. He is motivated by his fear – that I am bigger and stronger, and that I will best him without so much as breaking a sweat. But he is three times the size I am! What am I to do?"

Now, Fionn's natural and magical gifts may have been great, but he had one further advantage over any angry giant. Can you guess what that was? It was his wife.

If Fionn was clever, his wife was three times clev-erer. If he was tricksy, she was tricksier by far. And if Fionn was brave, she was braver than her husband and all the Fianna put together.

"Go outside," she said. "And come back when you see the giant coming. I'll ready everything in here."

Fionn went out, and he saw that the sunny day had grown dark, as though storm clouds had covered the sun. He ran up a hill nearby and scanned the horizon on every side. Then he saw what had caused the darkening of the day. The Scottish giant was walking from the west, and he was so tall and so broad that he had blotted out the sun. The very earth shook as he walked. Fionn turned and ran.

Back in the house, Fionn saw that his wife had brought a cradle from the sleeping floor into the middle of the great hall. She held out a fluffy knitted blanket and a white bonnet of her own.

"The giant is right behind me!" he cried. "What are you doing with that cradle? Where's my armour? Where's my shield?"

"Calm yourself, MacCumhaill," said his wife. "Put on this bonnet and let me wrap you in this blanket. Then climb into the cradle and close your eyes. I'll handle the giant."

Fionn opened his mouth to object, but then he

heard a dreadful knock at the door and he decided to trust his wife. He let her bundle him into the blanket and squeezed himself into the cradle. Then he jammed the bonnet on to his head and pretended to be asleep.

Fionn's wife sat down with her weaving loom and beckoned to a serving girl to open the door. "Welcome," she called to the Scottish giant. "Do come in."

The giant bent almost double and turned sideways to fit in through the door.

"Never mind your welcome, woman," growled the giant. "I've come for Fionn MacCumhaill. Where is he?"

"Whisht!" said Fionn's wife, and she put a finger to her lips. "I've just got my baby off to sleep. Please don't wake him up."

The giant looked shame-faced. "Sorry," he said in a whisper that would carry across at least three counties. "Where is Fionn?"

"He's gone to France," said Fionn's wife. "To fetch me some silken thread to weave a belt. He left this morning and he won't be back till evening."

"Evening?" said the giant. "Tonight?" Inwardly he was thinking, *What sort of man could make it to*

France and back in one day on foot? Fionn MacCumhaill must truly be the giant everyone says he is.

"You're welcome to wait," said Fionn's wife. "In the meantime, I'm going to make some scones. Sit down at the table and take off your boots, you've come a long way."

Fionn's wife made great scones the size of millstones. When she rolled out the giant's scone, she pressed great rocks into the dough. She cooked it on the griddle and slid it off on to the table in front of him. The giant bit into it and howled as he crunched right into a stone and chipped great pieces out of his enormous teeth.

"Oh, the stones didn't hurt you, did they?" asked Fionn's wife. "Fionn always loves to crunch the stones. His teeth are so strong." She gave the sort of giggle she imagined a silly woman might.

"No, not at all," said the giant, although he winced and rubbed his mouth. "How old is the baby?" he asked politely, and nodded at the cradle.

"Eight weeks," said Fionn's wife. "Come and meet him."

The giant tiptoed across to the cradle, the house shaking with every step.

"He's also called Fionn," said Fionn's wife proudly.

"What a fine lad," said the giant. "So . . . big. Eight weeks old, you say? So no teeth yet." He stuck his finger in Fionn's mouth and Fionn bit down on it as hard as he could.

The giant jumped six feet in the air and howled as he hit his head on the roof-tree. He cradled his bloody thumb in his other hand.

"I'll tell you this, woman," he said, "if that's the baby, I don't ever want to meet the father. Thank you for the scone. It's been . . . a pleasure."

The giant turned on his heel and ran out of the house as fast as his legs would carry him.

Fionn leaped out of the cradle and ran to the door. He caught the barest of glimpses of the Scottish giant, disappearing over the mountains in his speed to get home.

The Scottish giant never returned. He had met his match – in Fionn MacCumhaill's wife!

How Oisean Outlived the Fianna

In Gaelic manuscripts from Scotland and Ireland and in the traditions carried by storytellers in both countries, there are many stories of the great warband called the Fianna and their leader, Fionn MacCumhaill. These stories belong to both Scotland and Ireland, because for centuries the two countries shared a language and culture, and poets and storytellers travelled across the Irish Sea in both directions carrying stories and songs. This story uses many of the same characters, including Oisean, Fionn's son.

In this version of the story, Oisean's blessings for his friends come from the Gaelic song Tàladh

Dhòmhnaill Ghuirm, or Donald Gorm's Lullaby. Say "Oshan", "Neev", "Oscar' and "Coil-tcha".

Long, long ago there lived a band of strong and fearless warriors in Scotland who were called the Fianna. The Fianna roamed all across the Highlands and to and fro between Scotland and Ireland, where all the other Gaelic-speaking peoples lived. By day they honed their skills with weapons, fought their battles, and hunted for their food, and when night came they gathered together around the fire to feast and drink and make merry. Among their number was one who was a great bard and storyteller. He was Oisean, the son of Fionn MacCumhaill, and he had the finest voice and the best songs, the strongest memory for stories and the greatest gift for poetry. His songs of home and longing brought tears to the eyes of hardened warriors. His stories could make the fiercest fighter shudder and look about him as he settled into his blankets in the dark of the night. Above all, there was no greater honour for any hero than to have his valorous exploits recorded in one of Oisean's great praise-poems, to be sung far and wide long after he had ceased to live.

One day Oisean and other members of the Fianna were roasting fish on a fire beside a great loch when they heard hoofbeats approach. When the horse drew closer they saw that the rider was a woman – the most beautiful woman that any of them had ever seen.

The woman came down from her horse and stepped among them.

"I am Niamh," she said, "and I have come from Tìr nan Òg, the Land of the Ever Young. I have come to look for a man to marry from among the Fianna. We have no king in our land, and I am tired of ruling alone. I hear there are no stronger or braver men on Earth than the Fianna of Fionn MacCumhaill."

From the moment Oisean had seen the woman and heard her speak, he had known in the marrow of his bones that he would marry her. Among his great store of stories were many of Tìr nan Òg, and he had long yearned to see that place, where no one grows old and no lack or want is ever known. He stood up and took a deep breath to steady his heart.

"I will marry you," he said, and he reached his hand out to the woman. "I am not the fiercest warrior nor the boldest chieftain among the Fianna, but you will never feel the time long when I am by your side. I will move your heart with my songs and tickle your ribs with my stories. I will praise you in my poems for as long as we both shall live."

Niamh smiled. "That would please me well," she

said. "For in Tìr nan Òg we have all of the time in the world to fill."

The next few days were bittersweet for the Fianna. They would never again count such a great bard or storyteller among their number, and they knew that in the nights to come when they gathered round the fire, they would feel his loss. But his joy warmed their fierce old hearts and they were happy for him.

The wedding was an occasion of great mirth and merriment, with feasting and jousting, songs and laughter. Then the time came for Oisean to part with the Fianna.

"*Osgar euchdaich*," he said. "Worthy Osgar. *Gun robh neart na cruinne leat, 's neart na grèine.* May all the strength of the world be yours, and the strength of the sun."

Then he stepped up to Caoillte.

"*Chaoillte chalma*," he said, "Brave Caoillte. *Neart an tairbh dhuibh leat, as àirde a leumas.* May all the strength of the black bull be yours, that leaps the highest."

Like that he bid farewell to each and every one of his friends. Then Oisean and Niamh took their leave of the Fianna, climbed on the back of Niamh's white mare, and rode into the loch.

Tìr nan Òg was exactly as Niamh had promised, and even better. Oisean had his choice of every good thing to eat, and his fill to drink. There was no sickness or sadness there. Fruit grew on the trees, the air was scented with roasting meat and baking bread, and there was no sport or merriment he could not enjoy. For many years Oisean was the most contented man under the sun, together with his Niamh in that happy land.

One day Oisean was riding out on his mare when a small bird flew out from a tree and trilled its song. Oisean remembered hearing that song only once before, with the Fianna on the shores of Loch Lear in Scotland. Suddenly his heart was filled with longing to go back and see his friends one more time.

At first Oisean said nothing to Niamh of this longing, but Niamh was a loving wife and friend and she could see that all was not well with him.

"This is not a land where anyone should be sad," she said to Oisean one morning. "I know what ails you. You miss the Fianna. It's only natural – you lived among them for such a long time."

Oisean nodded. "I do miss them. But I knew when I came here that I would have to leave them behind."

Niamh smiled.

"It's all right," she said. "I'll let you have my white mare, the one that brought us here. She can swim through the waters of the loch where we were married and bring you to the land of mortal men. There is only one thing you must promise me. When you reach that land, whatever happens, you must not come down from the horse. If you do, she will never be able to bring you home again to me."

Oisean felt a great weight of sorrow lift from him and he beamed at Niamh. "Of course I promise," he said. "As soon as I have seen my friends, I'll come back here to you. This is my home now."

The next day Oisean bid farewell to Niamh, and climbed up on the back of the white mare to travel to the land of mortal men. They swam through the loch and came ashore in Scotland. It was the same place where he and Niamh had been married, but Oisean would not have recognized it had he not known it to be so. The great forests and pastures were gone and in their place were little towns and roads. No great herds of deer, no travelling bands of hunters. No Fianna. Nothing Oisean recognized at all.

Oisean understood then that time is different in Tìr nan Òg. For every happy year he had spent with Niamh there, dozens had passed in the land of mortal men. He had been gone perhaps a score of years, but hundreds had passed in Scotland. The Fianna were long gone.

"Hunt well, my friends," Oisean whispered to their memories, "in whatever eternal lands you roam now."

Oisean wiped his eyes and pulled on the horse's bridle to steer her back towards the loch. On the way they passed three men struggling to raise a great stone that blocked the road. They seemed so little and puny in comparison with the great warriors of Oisean's memory that he almost laughed. Then he felt unkind, and so he leaped off the horse to help.

As soon as Oisean felt the soil of Scotland under his feet once more, a strange feeling came over him. Too late he remembered the promise he had given Niamh. The white mare turned and fled towards the loch. The stone-movers gaped at Oisean with concern that turned to horror. Oisean felt his skin crinkle and wrinkle and the teeth grow loose in his mouth. His long hair turned white and his heartbeat began to pain him. He could no longer stand and, as he fell, the three men were at last released from the spell that had bound them and ran to help.

The men carried Oisean to a small cot-house nearby and sent for a holy man to bless him. The holy man came and gave Oisean the last rites as his eyes closed for the last time.

This story is told in Ireland and in Scotland. In Ireland the holy man who blesses Oisean is a young monk called Patrick, who became the great man known today as Ireland's patron saint. In Gaelic the story is called *Oisean às dèidh na Fèinne*, or "Oisean after the Fianna". Do you know the feeling of being "a fish out of water"? If a Gaelic speaker feels that way, they might use the name of this story to describe their situation. In this way people still remember Oisean's loneliness when he came home and found that his friends were gone for ever.

Fir Black

Sometimes people weave stories to explain the world. The Northern Lights, for example, are caused by charged particles from the sun striking atoms in Earth's atmosphere, which causes changes to electrons in the atoms that release energy that appears as light. Before scientists worked this out, people told a story instead that the Northern Lights were dancing angels, fallen from heaven.

This Gaelic story explains how Scotland's ancient forests disappeared and how, in some places, peat appeared in their place. It is not true – in fact, humans cut down much of Scotland's forest to make way for farming, and the peat formed as a result.

Long, long ago, before people first came to live in Scotland, the land was covered with trees. From north to south and from east to west, the great Caledonian forest grew from coast to coast and across the islands. Many species of tree flourished in these dense woodlands, but the keystone of the whole forest was the Scots pine. These branching, regal trees soared to over thirty metres tall and lived for hundreds of years. They gave food and shelter to squirrels and capercaillies, wildcats and pine martens and many more of the birds, animals and insects that made the great forest their home.

Today Scotland still has huge tracts of woodland, in Perthshire and Argyll, around the great rock where Stirling Castle sits, in the vast Cairngorms National Park and across the West Highlands. But these forests represent only a small fraction of the great Caledonian forest, and today some areas of Scotland have no trees at all.

In many of the places where no trees grow, the land lies under a blanket of peat. Peat is formed in waterlogged conditions, where plant and other natural material does not rot completely, but instead grows to cover the ground as a dense, dark substance that can be cut, dried and burned as fuel.

Sometimes, when people cut peat for their fires, they find the roots, trunks and branches of great trees, still whole but blackened and twisted after hundreds of years in the ground. These are the remnants of trees from the ancient forest and for hundreds of years people have told stories of how they ended up there, buried deep in the dark of the peat bogs.

It is said that the King of Lochlann looked with a jealous eye to Scotland, such a near neighbour, and yet not a friendly one. He saw the great forests and the strong, supple wood the Scottish king had at hand to make fine ships and great houses. When the Scots felled the trees to build their boats and their houses, they planted crops and grazed their animals in the clearings, and in the mild climate of Scotland, they flourished. Life was not so easy in Lochlann. There was a scarcity of land and the weather was cruel, and men and women and children died of hunger every year. Some years the animals perished, meaning the people had no milk or meat or wool, or new young animals to look forward to come spring. There were plenty of trees, but these were little and hardy, made for building sturdy boats that would stand up to rough seas. The people of Lochlann were the greatest seafarers in the world. Imagine if they had access to the great, soaring trees of Scotland, the king thought bitterly. Where could they *not* go then?

Eventually the King of Lochlann became so eaten up with jealousy that he made himself ill and took to his bed. The queen saw how it was and sent for her daughter Donan. Donan was a wise woman with a gift for herbs and healing. She had other gifts too that meant she could see straight through to what ailed the heart.

Donan gave her father every medicine she knew of, but he grew no better. Then Donan tried every little spell she knew to take the weight of sorrow from his mind, but that didn't work either. In the end she fell to her knees and wept.

"Is there nothing I can do, Father?" she asked. "Tell me what I can do to cure you. I'll try anything."

Her father's eyes opened a crack. "Anything?" he whispered.

"Anything," said Donan.

"Destroy the great forest of Scotland," her father said. "Leave not one tree standing. Then I'll be well again."

Donan's heart ached but she loved her father and could not bear to lose him. And so she turned herself into a great white bird, and flew across the sea to Scotland. When she reached the eastern fringes of the forest, she touched the trees with a wand clutched in the talons of her feet, and the forest burst into flames. Donan flew home to Lochlann and rested for seven days and seven nights.

The king grew a little better.

After a week had passed, Donan once again flew to Scotland. She saw that the eastern edge of the forest was gone, but the north and south, the west and the deep, dark heart stood strong. And so Donan flew to the south and struck the trees with her wand as she flew by. The southernmost edge of the forest was soon ablaze.

There was a great rustling and crying as the animals and the birds fled for their lives from the burning forest. Donan saw this happen and landed here and there to help any animal trapped by the flames.

The people living at the forest's edge were also forced to flee. They took their beasts and their possessions, but of course they could not take their oats or their barley from the fields. Those burned along with the forest.

"We'll have a hard winter this year," the people

wept. "With no homes and no grain to feed ourselves or our flocks."

A child pointed to the sky. "Look at that great bird up there in the trees! What is it?"

The people looked up and saw Donan flying here and there above the trees. She was bigger than any bird they had ever seen before, and white no longer, but blackened and sooty from the smoke of the fire.

Donan was seen again and again in the weeks that followed. The people called her "Fir Black", and soon they came to see that wherever she appeared, the great fires followed.

"We must stop Fir Black," the people said to one another. "Before the entire forest is gone."

They tried with bows and arrows to shoot Donan down, but she flew too high and the arrows fell short every time. The people busied themselves putting out the fires as best they could, digging trenches and cutting gaps in the forest to stop the terrible spread. All the while they talked about Fir Black, and how to stop her.

"She has a kind heart, I think," one little girl said. "I saw her save a nest of birds."

"A kind heart!" the adults scoffed. "When she has

destroyed our forest! Be quiet, little girl, and let us talk. We need to work out how to stop her."

But the little girl would not be quiet. "I think she cares for the animals," she said. "And that's how we could tempt her down."

And so, when Donan appeared in the skies on the western edge of the forest, the people were ready. They took the calves from the cows, the lambs from the ewes, and the kids from the mother goats. The air filled with cries of distress.

Donan looked down from the skies but the tree-cover was too great and she could not see what had caused the great howl of distress across the land. She saw a clearing ahead and came down to land. In that instant, an arrow shot up and pierced her heart, and she fell dead to the ground.

When the people gathered around Fir Black, they saw that she was a bird no longer, but a beautiful, black-haired woman whose fine gown was touched with soot. She had a golden circlet in her hair, golden bracelets on her arms and golden brooches on her shoulders. They had heard tell of Donan, the witch-daughter of the King of Lochlann, and now they understood that it was she they saw before them.

When the king heard of his daughter's death, he went almost mad with grief. He put to sea at once in his great dragon-ship, but a dreadful storm kept him from landing in Scotland to fetch her home. Instead the people of Scotland buried her on the hillside where she fell, beside Little Lochbroom in Wester Ross, and they named the place in memory of the woman who almost brought about the destruction of the great Caledonian forest.

A Note for Grown-ups

(AND ENQUIRING YOUNG MINDS)

I have had the privilege of hearing the stories in this collection from many great storytellers, and of reading others in the collections of iconic folklorists. In retelling them, I have aimed to treat them with the respect they deserve, and to balance this with – I hope – sensitive alterations to help unlock this magical literature to young readers of today.

I have added information here and there, particularly in the stories from Gaelic tradition, to help a modern child imagine themselves into the Highlands and islands of yesteryear. I have occasionally taken content away. In the modern world we associate fairy tales with children and young people, but this is not a true representation of the way they were traditionally told, and removing elements of adult content lets children enjoy the tales too.

Tales live in their tellers. The Gaelic proverb says,

A' chiad sgeul air fear an taighe, is sgeul gu latha air an aoigh.

It is for the host to tell the first tale, and the guest to tell stories till dawn.

Acknowledgements

Books are a team effort and first thanks are due to all at Scholastic, and especially to Jenny Glencross for all of her meticulous, kind and thoughtful editorial work. Our traditional tales are also a collective endeavour, passed down the generations and collected for future readers and listeners by the good efforts of fieldworkers and folklorists who recognised that Scotland had one of the great oral traditions of Europe and had the foresight to preserve it. I'm grateful to the many tellers and collectors from whom I learned these beautiful stories in person, in print and in the sound archives of the School of Scottish Studies. Clach air bhur càrn. Last thanks go to my wonderful husband Tom Morgan-Jones, who kept body and soul together while I worked on this dream of a project.

Also available from Scholastic Children's Books:

Read on for an extract...

Fionn and the Salmon of Knowledge

Near Tara, the seat of the High King of Ireland, flowed the River Boyne. According to legend, a magical fish called the Salmon of Knowledge was said to swim in its waters. Whoever was first to taste the flesh of this fish would have access to the wisdom of the world.

This is the story of the man who ate the Salmon of Knowledge, and used his new power to become one of Ireland's greatest heroes.

Once upon a time, a baby called Deimne was born to a very frightened mother called Muirne. She was hiding because her husband, Cumhall, had been murdered by a one-eyed warrior called Goll. He had killed Cumhall to take his place as leader of the Fianna, an elite group of warriors that guarded the king. Goll vowed to hunt down Cumhall's baby so that he wouldn't grow up to avenge his father's death.

Muirne knew her baby wouldn't be safe with her, so she left him to be raised by handmaidens in the wilds of the Slieve Bloom Mountains.

Deimne was a beautiful baby, with hair as fair as his father's. His handmaidens taught him all the ways of the wild. By the time he was a boy, Deimne could hunt a bird from the sky with a slingshot, and outpace a running deer.

As he got older he sought out company his own age, and one day was lured to the fort of a chieftain by a game of hurling being played by a group of boys. They asked Deimne his name, but the women who cared for him had told him it would be dangerous to reveal his name so he said nothing. So, the boys called him Fionn, which means "fair", because he had hair as golden as sheaves of wheat.

Fionn was given a hurley stick and taught the rules of the game. He picked it up quickly and soon became the best on the pitch. When he returned home, he told the handmaidens how the boys had called him Fionn. They liked the name and started calling him Fionn too. Having a new name might also keep the boy safe from Goll.

Each day, Fionn turned up to play hurling with the boys, and soon word spread about the strength, speed and bravery of this blond-haired boy.

The news reached the ears of Goll, the one-eyed captain of the Fianna who had killed Fionn's father.

"Did you say this boy has fair hair?" Goll asked the messenger.

The messenger nodded. "Yellow, like butter."

Cumhall also had fair hair, thought Goll. *Could this be the child I've been searching for?*

Goll sent his men to capture the boy.

Like Goll, the handmaidens had heard people talking about the blond-haired boy who was brilliant at hurling. They were worried about his safety, so they told him how his father, Cumhall, had once been the leader of the Fianna but had been killed by Goll.

Everyone knew about the Fianna, and Fionn was excited by the possibility of becoming one of them.

"Does that mean I am the rightful leader of the Fianna?" he asked.

The women nodded but told him he needed to become a warrior himself, before he became a captain of warriors. So, Fionn left their care to train with different chieftains in Ireland. He learned how to swing a sword, throw a spear and use a shield to defend himself. Soon he became one of the greatest warriors in the land, gathering his own band of followers, some of whom had been his father's old friends.

Fionn returned to his foster mothers to show off his hard-won battle skills.

"Am I now ready to become leader of the Fianna?" he asked.

"You are indeed a great warrior, Fionn," they said, "but a leader needs to be wise as well as dangerous."

They sent him to the banks of the River Boyne to learn the arts of poetry and storytelling from a wise man called Finnegas.

For seven years, the druid had been fishing in the river in the hope of catching the legendary Salmon of Knowledge. It was said that whoever ate the flesh of this fish would acquire all of the wisdom and knowledge of the world.

Over the seven years he had sought the fish, Finnegas had tried many different methods to catch it, but none had been successful.

Fionn took to his new training quickly. It was certainly easier than the fighting practice he'd undergone with the chieftains. Each morning, Fionn would collect dry wood. Once he had a fire going, he would gather wild fruit, nuts and herbs to be used in the dinner, later that day. Then he would check the fishing lines that Finnegas had set up along the river. He always expected to see the magical salmon dangling from a hook, but mostly he found nothing. If he was lucky he'd find a trout, which he'd gut and clean, and have ready for cooking later on.

Then he would do his study – usually memorizing a poem or story that Finnegas had recited the previous day. Fionn would practise retelling it aloud, while walking up and down the riverbank.

He wouldn't have thought this would be tiring, but after a few hours he always needed a break. Perhaps it was as tiring as training with weapons, but in a different way.

His break would consist of cooking the fish that had been caught earlier. He would build a spit by pressing two Y-shaped branches into the ground on either side of the fire. Then he would skewer the trout on to a third branch and place it on the two Y-shaped branches above the flames. The fish would then be rotated slowly until it was cooked.

Fionn and Finnegas would share the meal of trout, nuts and herbs. Afterwards, Finnegas would recite a new poem or story for Fionn to memorize the following day.

Student and teacher would sleep under the stars, with the sound of the river lulling them to sleep. It was a peaceful, if uneventful life.

One day, Fionn was busy composing a poem when he heard his teacher shouting his name from further down the riverbank. Fionn ran to the old man to see what was the matter. He found Finnegas dancing with joy, holding a huge red-speckled salmon, its scales glittering silver like the moon and its eyes full of wisdom.

"I caught it, my boy!" he shouted. "I finally caught the Salmon of Knowledge."

"That's fantastic news," said Fionn. "What will you do with it?"

Finnegas laughed. "Eat it, of course."

"Shall I cook it for you, master?" asked Fionn. "Or would you prefer to cook this one yourself."

"You've become rather good at the cooking, my boy. So yes, I'd like you to do it." He handed the fish over. "But you must swear that you won't taste the flesh before me."

"I promise," said Fionn.

"Not even the smallest bite," warned Finnegas. "I must be the first to eat it."

Fionn nodded and built a fire, placed the salmon on a spit and then hung it over the flames. The smell of the cooking fish, and the sight of its crisp, golden skin made Fionn's mouth water, but he was a man of his word and kept his promise not to take even a small bite of the salmon.

As Fionn turned the spit, he thought about what it would be like to have all the knowledge of the world. You would always know which direction to take in the woods, which weapon to choose in a fight, and when your enemy was next going to attack. It was a power that could make you very popular with every king in Ireland. It was an ability that could make you a very rich ma—

"Ouch!" shouted Fionn.

He'd been so busy daydreaming that he hadn't been concentrating on the job at hand, and as he was turning the spit, he scorched his thumb on the hot salmon. Immediately, he put his thumb in his mouth to ease the pain. But sucking the throbbing blister on his thumb did more than ease the pain in his thumb – it also gave him the first taste of the fish.

Centuries of knowledge and wisdom flowed through his mind in a torrent of light, image and sound, and Fionn knew that something special had happened to him.

But instead of delight, he felt only guilt. Finnegas had spent years waiting to catch this salmon, and along comes a student and steals that honour away from him. How disappointed Finnegas would be. How betrayed he would feel.

Perhaps if I say nothing, thought Fionn, *and Finnegas eats the salmon, then he'll receive the gift as well as me.*

He decided not to tell Finnegas when he called him for his meal. However, as soon as the teacher saw Fionn, he noticed there was something different about his student. His eyes seemed brighter, deeper and . . . something else. They seemed wiser.

"Did you taste the salmon?" asked Finnegas, a nervous fear pulling at his face. He looked like he already knew the answer, but was hoping he was wrong.

Fionn swallowed the lump in his throat. He couldn't lie to his teacher. It was bad enough that he'd stolen the man's dreams away, without lying about it too.

He told Finnegas what had happened.

For a long time, Finnegas stared at the ground, speechless. But when he looked up, there was no anger in his eyes, only sadness.

"A prophecy said a fair-haired man would eat the Salmon of Knowledge," he said. "Because my hair was once blond, I thought that would be me, but seemingly not. The gift of knowledge is yours, Fionn, so please, eat the fish."

He handed over the steaming salmon and waited for his student to eat. Fionn, however, had lost his appetite.

"Please eat, my boy," said Finnegas. "Though I am a little sad not to be the chosen one, I am happy that the gift of knowledge has gone to a man of honour such as yourself."

Fionn Mac Cumhaill nodded, ate the fish and received the superpower that had eluded Finnegas for so long. From that day on, whenever Fionn wanted to know what the future held, or he was trying to solve some mystery, he merely had to put his scorched thumb in his mouth and whatever knowledge he required would always come to him. He promised himself that he would only use this power for the good of his fellow people and never for selfish reasons. It was this promise, rather than the power itself, that led Fionn to become one of Ireland's greatest heroes, loved by king and peasant alike.